RAISING
SAFETY-SMART
KIDS

RAISING SAFETY-SMART KITS

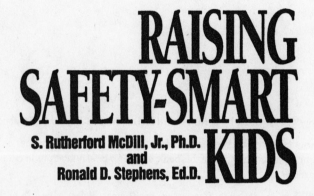

S. Rutherford McDill, Jr., Ph.D.
and
Ronald D. Stephens, Ed.D.

With:

David Stephens

T. J. Stephens

Leslie Stephens

Erin McDill

James Stephens

Lindsay McDill

Publishers Since 1798

THOMAS NELSON PUBLISHERS

Nashville

Case studies in this book, unless otherwise indicated, are from the authors' experiences. Names and other identifying information have been changed to protect the privacy of those involved.

Copyright © 1993 by S. Rutherford McDill, Jr., and Ronald D. Stephens.

All rights reserved. Written permission must be secured from the publisher to use or reproduce any part of this book, except for brief quotations in critical reviews or articles.

Published in Nashville, Tennessee, by Thomas Nelson, Inc., Publishers, and distributed in Canada by Word Communications, Ltd., Richmond, British Columbia, and in the United Kingdom by Word (UK), Ltd., Milton Keynes, England.

Scripture quotations are from the NEW KING JAMES VERSION of the Bible. Copyright © 1979, 1980, 1982, Thomas Nelson, Inc., Publishers.

Library of Congress Cataloging-in-Publication Data

McDill, S. R. (S. Rutherford)
    Raising safety-smart kids / S. R. Brik McDill, Jr. ; contributors, David Stephens ... [et al.].
        p.   cm.
    ISBN 0-8407-4141-3 (pbk.)
    1. Safety education. 2. Children's accidents—Prevention. 3. Child rearing.
I. Stephens, Ronald D. II. Title.
HQ770.7.M34   1993
649'.1—dc20   83-3740
                                                                       CIP

Printed in the United States of America

1 2 3 4 5 6 7 - 98 97 96 95 94 93

Contents

Dedication

This project is dedicated to our children Erin, Lindsay, David, Leslie, James, T.J.

The enterprise of raising them has been full of equal amounts of delight, challenge, hard work, fun, exasperation, laughter, frustration, suspense, sleepless nights (waiting for doctors to perform miracles), celebration, sober conversations, hilarity, fright, triumph, terror, elation, endless bills, pride, chagrin, natural consequences, rescues all rolled into that two decade adventure called parenthood.

It is to them we owe this book. They helped us write it, line by line, page by page, experience by experience.

We are gratified by their lives and personalities. We are better people for having had them come into our lives.

Thanks, guys. . . . (Now, can I have my car back?)

Acknowledgments

No book can be written without the help and support of a number of often unsung heroes, but we want to acknowledge the resource contributions of the National School Safety Center. We want to thank our families who gave unlimited and sometimes unmerited grace and understanding.

We especially want to thank Carol Lacy, a special friend and co-laborer in writing, who nurtured this project from start to finish. Carol, with her years in the industry and her gentle way, functioned in a number of vital roles—agent, critic, encourager, wordsmith, consultant, advisor, and most importantly, critically needed translator. She took pedagogical narrative and made it come alive.

Introduction

Once upon a time, and not so long ago, parents confidently sent children off to school, trusting that this extension of home was a good place to be. Mom and Dad saw school as a place of shelter, a safe harbor where their little ones were nurtured and protected from fearful giants, ogres, and dragons. After all, these threats were characters in fairy tales, dangers they believed their children would never encounter. Teachers would shape young, pliable minds with knowledge and values that would stay with them throughout their lives, molding them into productive members of society.

Of course, kids, being kids, always did some reckless things along the way that occasionally led them to the principal's office. But their adventures in rebellion were not life-threatening. The really "bad" kids ditched school for a day of illicit freedom or retreated to the hindermost part of the school playground for a quick puff on a cigarette stolen from Dad's dresser. They had fistfights, used dirty four-letter words, and cheated on their exams. In high school they might sneak a swig of beer or spike the punch at the Friday night sockhop. But these were exceptions to the general run of kids, especially those from active Christian homes.

The popularity of the TV show "Happy Days" reflected parents' hope that life still could be innocent and that the Richies, Ralphs, and Potsies really existed—alongside the worldly, cool Fonz in his carefully ironed T-shirt with sleeves rolled up to show off bulging biceps. Heyyyyyyy!

Today, gunfights have replaced fistfights, and fire drills are augmented by crisis drills and bullet drills. Experts warn us to brace ourselves for an even greater groundswell of juvenile crime as today's kindergartners reach adolescence. Nearly three million crimes occur on school campuses each year. That's almost sixteen thousand every school day, or one every six seconds! Kids are getting harder, meaner, tougher, crueler, and more criminal-minded. Ann Landers, nationally syndicated columnist, reported that she had received more than twelve-thousand letters—and they were still coming—in response to a column about a family that had moved to Toronto because their children had been beaten up and robbed so often in a Boston school. [1]

Signs everywhere point to the prodigalizing of children whose parents came of age at the dawning of the "age of Aquarius." These '60s youngsters were admonished to "question authority," and they did so on college campuses, through neighborhood riots—anywhere they could get media attention. They were told to "turn on, tune in, drop out" by role models such as Timothy Leary, the high priest of LSD use.

Rap Brown's "burn baby burn" has once again become the motto of kids coming of age in the cruel and unforgiving inner city. The burning, looting, and violence of the 1992 Los Angeles riots in the wake of the Rodney King court decision exhibit this continuing trend. But anger, frustration, and fear are not confined to ghetto and barrio. The danger is spreading into nearly every corner of American life with rape, pillage, plunder, and murder becoming commonplace among the young.

We are horrified by statistics on youth "wildings"—one race pitted against another, minority against minority, gang against gang. For every incident that gets news coverage, scores— if not hundreds— of wildings on elementary, middle, and high school campuses, in residential neighborhoods, and on city streets are never reported.

This is only the tip of the iceberg. How can you as a parent prepare your children to cope with or steer clear of the giants, dragons, and ogres they will face in school, in the streets, and even in their own homes? Many families enroll their children in church-affiliated or other independent private schools in an attempt to protect them. But not every family can afford to send even one, much less two, three, or more children to private schools. Public schools remain their only option and the children must get there on their own.

Other families are turning to home study, but often both parents have to work during the day to survive inflation, making home learning difficult to supervise.

Most parents truly hope that the values they instill in their children will protect them from joining or fraternizing with gangs. Yet, "good" families find that their children are often friends with those whose values are not so worthy. Crime and violence are no respecters of race, religion, color, or affiliation. Children are often bullied, beaten, and victimized at school or on the way to school. And even the best and most dedicated families sometimes lose their children to other value systems when they stray from the paths their parents start them on.

Keeping kids away from trouble and keeping trouble away from kids are the issues this book addresses. You *can* protect your child from bullies, gangs, drugs, racism, and sexual abuse in the classroom, at parks, playgrounds, beaches, movie theaters, malls, and in the streets, and from dangers in their own homes. You *can* help your child build positive self-esteem that will help him resist the lure of gang membership.

You do not have to move from your familiar neighborhood, or even to a different city, to protect the welfare of your children. Even though we live in an unsafe world, we do not need to live with the constant worry, apprehension, and fright that constrict growth and stunt development. Those who are overwhelmed by this kind of anxiety become focused on the disappointment and frustration of what they cannot do rather than on the excitement and adventure of what they can do. Life becomes a scary patrol through dangerous enemy territory with the psychological wear and tear of constant vigilance and defensiveness.

Within each chapter of this book is a section entitled "What Works," devoted to our own children's thoughts, opinions, and recommendations. They talk about what worked for them, what did not, what kept them on the right track and out of harm's way. We felt this aspect of the book was important enough to bundle our children together for an intensive weekend writing retreat (one even flew home from Europe just for the weekend). All of them had read this manuscript in preparation for their input, and we asked them to be brutally honest and direct, no holds barred. We were a bit nervous about what they might say, but you can read the results for yourself:

"As kids of the authors, we were sheltered from many major problems of the inner cities, but all children everywhere go through some of the trials this book talks about. Our fathers asked the six of us to contribute our thoughts on how to help kids be 'safety smart.' The 'What Works' and 'What Doesn't Work' sections are the results of our weekend retreat to a special hideaway, a small table, ten pads of paper, fifteen pens and pencils, and eight meals from McDonalds. We believe this book is worthwhile, and we hope you do, too."

Your children can become *safety-smart* if you prepare, protect, prevent, and invest time with them in fostering the skills and abilities necessary for their success.

1

How to Begin

Each child brings special hope and promise as he or she enters the world. Filled with precious optimism, new mothers and fathers do not want to think about the bad things that could happen on a child's way to maturity. They feel confident that they can protect their helpless offspring from dangers that threaten. In those areas where they feel they need help, most new parents look for guidance from their own parents, pediatricians, and books on child-rearing. These teachers tell about nutrition, potty training, social interaction, preparation for school, right-brain/left-brain development, cleanliness, how to survive an earthquake or other natural disaster, how to cross the street, stranger danger, and how to avoid "bad" kids.

Preparing a child to cope in a violent world also means you have to give him a lot of inner support. This kind of training begins at birth. As Mother's Joy and Father's Pride matures, the child will grow through several distinct and qualitatively different stages before she finally reaches adulthood.

Biologically, a child develops from an uncoordinated, gangly preschooler (birth to five years) who can barely control basic biological functions, to an early school-age (six to ten years), whirling dervish with enough energy to power three adults. Then for a while (ages eleven to thirteen) he will settle down just a little as the body readies itself for the hormonal upheaval of heretofore unexperienced proportions.

If your child is to grow into a responsible adult who can care for himself, the child must be propped up, supported, and encouraged throughout this whole growing-up period. These supports include nurturing, cherishing, and valuing your child; giving him love, warmth, affection, and encouragement; forgiving him and making him feel needed, and protecting him in a safe home environment.

Children Should Be Nurtured and Cherished

Children have strong appetites for attention and an innate need for others to care for them. Their first cries are for someone to respond to and meet their needs.

Contrary to some authorities, parents should lavish on their newborn children all the physical and psychological attention they need. The strictures of limits, schedules, and boundaries should not be a part of a child's first year of life. Disciplinary values can be introduced later. Psychological nurturing begins with the warmth that comes from the mother's breast and continues as the mother holds, rocks, talks, and hums to her child as he drifts to sleep with a satisfied stomach.

This need to be nurtured never disappears. While physical demands for feeding and comfort may change, the need to feel special and cherished never goes away. It is the glue that holds a person together, that makes life worthwhile. It is the soul food of childhood. Without it, children's souls wither and shrivel into crinkled shells— dry, thin, and parched into nothingness.

A child who is nurtured, nourished, and cherished in his own family will become his own centered person who probably will not fall victim to the strong pressures of peer groups as he moves through childhood and adolescence.

Children Need to Feel Valued

Children have an appetite for feeling important, valued, and worthy of recognition. "I am someone. I matter. I am valid. My existence matters."

As children mature, being validated as someone special becomes paramount. While the need is usually exhibited by showing off when the child is young, by the time he is school age it comes into clear focus. Every elementary teacher knows well the wide-eyed expression and waving raised hand that signals, "I know the answer. Please! Puhleeze call on me." The "me-too" yearning is felt most sharply when the child feels left out.

Children Need Love, Warmth, and Affection

Hearts and souls under construction need an atmosphere that bathes them with emotional warmth. Affection is the heart-to-heart, soul-to-soul, skin-to-skin, let-me-give-you-a-hug physical expression of that surrounding warmth. Every kid needs a full daily allotment. The more you give him, the better he is. This is one commodity you cannot give too much of. No child can ever be spoiled by too much love, warmth, and affection.

One essential part of showing affection is physical touch. Touch is critical to healthy development. A condition described as *marasmus*, a Greek word meaning "wasting away," was plaguing children in orphanages, hospitals, and homes during the late nineteenth and early twentieth centuries. Children who were getting plenty of food and medical attention were still wasting away and dying. In some orphanages the mortality rate was nearly 100 percent.

After extensive research, it was discovered that these children were suffering from a simple lack of physical contact. Caretakers were either too busy or unaware of the need every person has to be touched, caressed, patted, hugged, and held. Finally, their caretakers began to "mother" them every day—picking them up, carrying them around, and handling them several times each day. One hospital reported that the infant death rate fell from 35 percent to below 10 percent.[1]

This phenomenon was also discovered in the vast orphanages in Romania after the overthrow of the Ceausescu regime. Because of understaffing, none of the abandoned babies and children in Romanian orphanages had been given adequate physical touching—indeed, they received little care of any kind. Many had not even had diapers changed regularly, including children chronologically old enough to have been potty-trained.

One relief organization told about little Catalina. Abandoned by her parents who already had at least nine children, two-year-old Catalina looked and acted like a child of five or six months. She was virtually ignored in a room with twenty-three other children, one adult, and three toys. Even though she received food and shelter she could not walk, feed herself, or relate to people. Her greatest deprivation was never being touched, cuddled, caressed, or comforted. That changed when a Christian agency stepped in to offer help to the overworked Romanian staff, and a year later, little Catalina was a different child and eligible for adoption by an American family.[2]

The bumper sticker "Have you hugged your child today?" should be an effective reminder that our children need to be touched in love many times during every day.

When your child has received his minimum daily requirement of love, warmth, and affection he will, on his own, uncouple from you and enter his own self-guiding orbit, coming close again for emotional refueling when his tanks run low. Your responsibility is to be close at hand and available day or night when your child needs refueling. If he sees a "closed" sign he will seek emotional sustenance somewhere else perhaps not as wholesome or safe as the home front. And there are plenty of eager and not-so-honorable sources of emotional sustenance ready to exploit those who crave what they cannot get at home. None of us ever outgrows the lifelong need for warmth and affection.

An encouraging by-product of being ready, willing, able, and eager to give your children emotional warmth and affection is that they *will* automatically internalize, as if by osmosis, *your* moral values as they cozy and cuddle next to you during refueling.

Children Need Encouragement

As your children mount up on their small and shaky eaglet wings they need your support and encouragement. Their healthy development calls for your proud words of praise and commendation. They will be critical enough of themselves—quick self-criticism goes hand-in-hand with childhood and adolescence. They need your cheers and acclaim to continue moving forward in the face of their own, sometimes intense, discouragement and self-belittlement.

Children and adolescents take many painful belly flops. They are self-conscious, socially awkward, and ungainly during their teen years, and they need your soothing words of esteem to know that their pain and mortifying embarrassment are not permanent.

Kids naturally gravitate toward those whose opinion of them is high. The world is full of enticing pied pipers whose slick and seductive snares seek to trap children. With a few well-chosen words of acclamation, you can soothe, attract, and hold your kids closer to you. You can encourage and guide them through some pretty perilous passages. By nature kids tend to reject parental guidance, so why not do what the crafty enticers of the world do so cunningly—package your guidance in character-building words of praise.

Children Need to Be Forgiven

Childhood and adolescence are times of mistake-making, growth, and mid-flight correction. The tasks involved in growing up are those that stretch children's wings. Their lives are organized around the dynamic of wanting to do what the next stage of development permits them to do. Their wishes and drives are often one lap ahead of their actual level of development, while their proven skills are one lap behind. They will blunder and stumble along on that slippery ground between, making mistakes as they go. They should have the luxury to err without I told you so's adding insult to their mortified egos.

Freely offered forgiveness provides a warm blanket of comfort when fragile self-esteem is injured. Children and adolescents should always feel that they can turn to non-critical parents for help and assistance. They may never express gratitude in words, but their thoughts will be, "Thank you for being sensitive and understanding during that disaster. Thanks for forgiving me when I embarrassed or disappointed you. Thanks for not lecturing me."

When you as parents can create that kind of atmosphere, you can rest assured that your children will seek *your* help in times of trouble. When turmoils and terrors in the school and the streets threaten their well-being, they will feel free to share their concerns with you openly, without fearing condemnation, ridicule, or criti-cism.

Children Need to Feel Needed

Children need to feel that their parents are as concerned about relating with them as they are in building relationships with people outside the family. They want to feel important and special to their parents. When you treat them as someone special, your relationship will take on higher levels of mutual and reciprocal caring, respect, and sensitivity. They will see you practicing what you preach and will act out what you teach them by example. You will not have to worry about what they are doing when you are not around.

Children Need to Feel Protected in a Safe Home Front

A deep sense of physical and psychological safety and protec-tion allows a new baby to settle in and develop. Life is supposed to be a meaningful and fulfilling enterprise where a child's mind climbs to unknown heights. Children are supposed to soar with eagles, developing wings of strength and power. They should not have to hunker down, scared to death in some sequestered corner, afraid to venture out lest they get blown away verbally or physically by hostile or even "friendly" fire. A parent who can instill in a child a sense of being protected and safe equips this child with the strength and courage to chase venturesome dreams and wildly crazy schemes that only a child can imagine without being afraid of danger lurking, lightning striking, or snipers firing.

A child's home front should be innately and inherently safe. He should feel more safe and secure at home than anyplace else. Home should be the one place where he can let down his guard, his armor, his defense. Home should be a sanctuary, a place of rest, restoration, healing, and safety.

Healthy psychological, personality, and ego development call for a safe, secure environment in which to try new wings. First flight needs calm, stable air; as new wings become stronger they will develop the kind of strength that can cope with turbulence. Your job as a parent is to provide your children with that protected setting. It is your profound responsibility to be a constructive part of that brave unfolding. Providing protected, secure airspace for their flight practice is essential. Giving your children these early props will almost guarantee their coping ability in a not always joyful world.

What Works

Every child wants to feel special, valued.

1. Give us little no-fail jobs that will build our pride:
   Carry marshmallows on trips.
   Carry bricks on work days (or other easily achieved tasks).
   Handle Dad's tools.
   Clean Dad's electric razor.
   Scratch Mom's back (physical contact).

2. Provide ways that will teach us self-worth:
   Go on a parent-child outing without other siblings.
   Get special cards on ordinary days.
   Be designated "present wrapper," "beater licker," "vege table platter arranger."

Be asked to comment on Mom's and Dad's parenting
practices/techniques.
Actively participate in family meetings.
Help us feel we can tell you anything (almost!).

3. Help us get involved in healthy activities and make it
    possible to continue in them:
    Drive us to practice.
    Make time for us, don't *find* it.

4. Forgive us our trespasses:
    It's okay to spill milk. Accidents are allowed.
    Tell us when we're wrong, but love us anyhow.
    It's okay to spank within limits.
    Mom and Dad should agree on discipline and be
    consistent with punishment.
    Help us to experience both winning and losing. Don't
    protect us all the time.

What Doesn't Work

1. Remember that we learn 100 percent by example:
    Don't tell us to "do as I say, not as I do." If you don't
    want us to smoke or drink, don't you do it.
    As grown-up kids, we find ourselves more like our parents
    than we ever thought we would be. We're great copiers!

2. Don't encourage competition between siblings:
    Give every child the right to his or her individuality.
    Don't expect us all to be the same.
    If we don't get straight *A'* s, find other things we're good
    at.

PART I

Home Alone

2

The Latchkey Child

A "latchkey child" is one who is regularly left without adult supervision for several hours each day. The term is a hangover from the nineteenth century when children from the poorer classes wore their house keys around their necks.

Sixty percent of all children in the United States under thirteen years old are left alone for several hours each day because their parents (or parent in single-parent families) work outside the home.[1] Their parents are in all economic classes—low-income to higher-income. During the school day the children may be left alone in the morning with the responsibility to get out of the house and to school on time. Then they return home after school to an empty house where they are expected to remain and stay out of trouble until their exhausted mother or father returns home. With little or no supervision, kids have only their imaginations to guide them, and their evolving biochemistry keeps them in almost constant emotional and physiological flux.

Parents assume that their kids have the emotional and intellectual maturity to know automatically how to use free time. They hope their children can plan things so that everything happens that should and nothing happens that shouldn't. However, anything that crops up that the child has never experienced can cause him to become confused and terrified.

Statistics indicate that the number of latchkey children will not decrease. Single-parent families are becoming more prevalent because of the high divorce rate, unwed teen mothers, and families separated through various intrusions. However, latchkey children also come from two-parent homes where mothers work because of necessity or choose to resume working after they have children. Statistics reveal that at least 52 percent of women with children under three years of age work away from home.[2]

There are several avenues you can take to ensure the safety of your most prized possessions. The first avenue, of course, is to consider whether you can scale down your lifestyle so that one parent can remain at home. Another consideration, if you must work, is to see if your budget would allow hiring competent help. Some employers are finding value in providing child-care at the workplace. A third avenue is to investigate after-school programs that your school offers or can implement. Community organizations may also offer solutions to working parents.

If you cannot stay home with your children, or hire someone to be with them at home, or find proper, affordable day care for them while you are at work, there are ways to better ensure their safety if they must be home alone.

Danger from the Intruder

Kevin, the fictitious eight-year-old in the film *Home Alone* who was accidently left behind when his family flew off for a Christmas European trip, was played as pretty savvy when burglars broke into his house. He set up booby traps throughout the house before the burglars knew he was there, and contrived swinging hazards that effectively slowed up the two bumbling burglars. However, most children of this age would not be so clever or so able to cope with such a traumatic experience—nor would they be faced with such inept criminals.

Parents feel that if a child stays in the house with the doors locked, he or she will be safe and protected from the dangers outside. Often, however, the danger breaks into the house or is already in there when your child gets home.

Jenny arrived home from school about the same time as usual. As she unlocked the front door she got that same anxious feeling in the pit of her stomach she always got when she had to go into the house alone. Nothing had ever happened, but she always felt a little afraid. As she started into the dining room she came face to face with a man carrying a box. She was so startled she didn't scream or run. She just stood there, frozen, staring into his face.

The man dropped the box, grabbed Jenny, and smacked his hand over her mouth. Jenny struggled to get loose, but the man was far too strong for her. He dragged her into the kitchen, snatched up a dishtowel, and crammed it into her mouth. Then, still tightly holding on to the squirming child, he ripped the telephone cord out of the wall and bound her arms and legs with it. Jenny's wide, terrified eyes never left his face as he completed his burgling. He knew she would never forget what he looked like, so as he was leaving the house, he waved a knife at her and threatened to come back and kill her and her parents if she ever told anyone what he looked like. Jenny lay on the floor, tears flowing from her eyes.

When Jenny's parents came home, they found their house torn apart. Worse, they found their daughter lying on the kitchen floor, bound, gagged, and terrified.

Latchkey kids who spend a lot of time alone are especially vulnerable, and although they may never admit it, they harbor fears that someone will break in and rob their home and perhaps harm them. Parents are responsible to see that their possessions— especially their children—are protected from the bad guys who are professional or even amateur burglars. In the book *Protect Your Home and Family,* author Ted Schwarz has helpful ideas on how you can effectively do this.

Schwarz suggests making your home safe—from the outside in. First, take a look at the possibility of getting inside without a key. We have all done this when we accidentally locked ourselves out—trying every door and window, hoping we had left one of them unsecured. A professional burglar does the same. But he doesn't bother to call a locksmith if he can't find a way in. He has in his possession all the tools he needs to break in. Check out your home:

- ☐ Do you have deadbolts on all the doors?
- ☐ Does any door have glass in it or to the side of it?
- ☐ Are any of your entrances hidden by shrubbery, a fence, or a wall?
- ☐ Does your apartment building have security?
- ☐ Do you have an alarm system?
- ☐ Do all of your windows lock—upstairs as well as downstairs?
- ☐ Do you live in a safe neighborhood?
- ☐ How well do you know your next-door neighbors?
- ☐ Does your front door have a peephole—a small viewing lens that fits into the door so that you can see who is standing outside before you open the door?
- ☐ If you rent, who else has a key to your house or apartment?[3]

How does your home rate on this break-in scale? Not many of us can claim to have a burglarproof house, so we should teach our children some precautions to help them keep safe. Go over the following rules with them. Have them practice them with you so that they become automatic.

- Never open the door to anyone when you are home alone. If an adult you know well—such as a relative—rings the doorbell, he or she may get upset if you don't open the door. But the general rule should be that no one gets in the house when you are home alone. Don't open the door even if the person claims to be a meter reader, the telephone repair person, a delivery person, or other service personnel. No service company allows its people to enter a house where no adult is present. Children should not open the door to them.

- If a package is being delivered by UPS, Express Mail, Federal Express, or any other delivery service, it should be left outside on the porch. Don't open the door to accept a package for your family or for a neighbor.

- Never admit someone who says he or she needs to use the telephone for any reason. If someone needs emergency help, you can call 911 for the person.

- If, when you get home from school, you see that the front door is unlocked or ajar, don't go in. Your first reaction may be, "Oh, no! I forgot to lock the door when I left." That may not be the case. Go to a neighbor's house and ask the neighbor to go inside with you or call the police.

- If you walk into the house and find things in disarray, or see anything suspicious, walk out the door and go to a neighbor's house.

- If you enter the house and catch a burglar in the act of carrying out the family's possessions, don't try to stop the burglary or keep him from escaping. Stay away from the doors and windows. Stay calm! Don't start screaming or running. Almost any burglar can outrun and outfight a child.

Making your house secure, and instructing your children in a few rules will help keep them safe in their own homes.

Danger from the Inside

Parents sometimes feel that there is greater safety in numbers, that if two or three children arrive home about the same time, especially if one is a teenager, there isn't much to be concerned about. They can tattle on each other, and they won't feel nervous about being alone. However, this sometimes creates other problems.

"Kelly," twelve, hates to go home after school. Her brother Michael, fourteen, is supposed to watch over her. But usually two or three friends come home with him.

A couple of years ago, when Kelly was ten, the boys started to touch her and rub her chest. She was very nervous about being touched, but she felt helpless and did not know what to do. Now that her body is beginning to develop, the boys want to reach under her blouse and feel her growing breasts. Not only that, Michael makes her let them touch her all over. Also, they force her to touch and feel them. She is beginning to be more afraid because the boys are getting rougher and more aggressive. But her fear only makes the boys more excited. They still are not making her do "it," but she knows it is only a matter of time until they do.

Kelly has started arriving home later and later. She goes to a girlfriend's house or hangs around school until one of the teachers sends her home. Her mother gets mad and yells at her for not being there when she calls the house. Once Kelly tried to explain to her mother why she didn't want to come home, but Michael overheard her and came into the room and stared at her with an unspoken threat. Kelly, afraid, shut up. Home is no longer a happy, safe place for Kelly.

To avoid such situations, parents need to:

- Create the kind of home where kids know they can speak openly and straightforwardly about what goes on and be protected by both parents, united.

- Every so often take one child at a time out to dinner and ask him to talk about home, school, and himself. Ask in a way that conveys sincerity. If anything should be changed, follow through and resolve the problem.

- Let your children know that you will protect the one who is being bullied, then follow through. Tell them you will not put up with this kind of intimidation.

Other Worries, Dangers, and Fears

Coming home and finding someone strange in the house or being exploited or intimidated by older siblings are not the only dangers children encounter in their own homes. Sometimes the danger is unwittingly put there by parents. Children often get into their parents' drugs or alcohol or try smoking their cigarettes. Sometimes children find firearms and practice shooting a supposedly empty gun.

Most latchkey children are not allowed to have friends over because they might become rowdy and get hurt and the parents would be responsible for injury to someone else's child. So most children turn to television for companionship. However, their selection of TV programs can add to children's anxiety and confuse their developing emotions. Children tend to watch shows their parents won't let them see when they are home. Some of these shows can contribute to imaginary or real fears that children are reluctant to discuss with parents because they do not want to be punished for doing something they were not supposed to do in the first place.

Kids worry about the house catching fire or someone breaking in to rob or kill them. They resent having to clean their rooms, do their homework, defrost the meat for dinner, feed the pets, rake the leaves, empty the trash, put the breakfast dishes in the dishwasher. . . . Parents seem to feel that the busier they can keep a latchkey child, the safer he is. This is not the case. These children feel abandoned, neglected, and imposed on.

Parents should provide stimulating activities, not just chores, that will encourage their child's social and emotional development. Being isolated from parents and friends even for a few hours every day often leads children to feel lonely, bored, frightened, rejected, and socially insecure. These feelings stay with them even after they are grown.

Lynette and Thomas J. Long, in *The Handbook for Latchkey Children and Their Parents*, say:

On the whole, latchkey children spend more time alone and less time with their friends than their parent-watched counterparts. Yet the elementary school years are a time when children learn how to interact with others. Children see their worth as how well they are respected in their peer group. Limiting those interactions (or exposing children to improper relationships) can reduce feelings of belonging and minimize feelings of self-worth. In addition, learning how to interact with and feel accepted by others is a primary task of childhood that affects how a child will interact with others in later life.[4]

Because of low self-esteem and the fact that they have not learned to relate properly with their peers, these children as they grow older may seek comfort in drugs, sex, gangs, crime, or strange and sometimes dangerous religious cults that offer acceptance, belonging, and affection.

Talk to Your Latchkey Child

Not only is it up to parents to clear away the known hazards and stake out a safe territory for their home-alone children, they also need to instruct children on how to take care of themselves, to set certain rules, and see to it that the children understand and accept those rules.

Ask your kids how they feel about being left alone. The first thing the youngest may say is, "Johnny bosses me all the time," or worse, a non-committal, dispirited "Okay." Children often have trouble verbalizing feelings. You might ask them to write down how they feel (if they are old enough to write that well) or draw pictures of themselves when they are alone. Once you know what they are afraid of or concerned about, then you can begin to deal with these feelings.

Talk about how it feels to come home to an empty house. Ask your child questions such as what he would do if he lost his key, found the door unlocked, or saw that a window had been broken.

Rather than ridicule or criticize wrong answers, teach him what he should do instead.

Encourage your child to keep a journal of his thoughts and activities when he is alone. Writing down fears and feelings helps a child to deal with them. Keeping track of how he spends his time when no one else is around can show him why he cannot finish his homework or chores. Maybe he escapes his boredom by watching TV, playing video games, or talking for hours on the phone. Kids on their own cannot think of fulfilling ways to use their time. They need guidance.

Map out some flexible rules together. These should include rules about using the telephone for social calls, having friends over, using electrical or gas appliances, using matches to light the fireplace, taking medicines, leaving the house or yard, and what to do if a stranger approaches the house or if there is an emergency. The rules should also outline regular chores your child is expected to do. Bear in mind that it is possible to overburden your child with too many jobs around the house.

Even the youngest child can learn how to use the telephone, including portable mobile phones. Important numbers should be posted on the refrigerator or tacked on the wall near the phone. At the top of the list is the 911 emergency number; next, your work numbers; then the number of a close neighbor, Grandma, or other relative who is home during the day, your doctor's office, etc.

Keep nutritious snacks in the house. Avoid too many sweets or other junk food. These sometimes cause nervous emotional highs followed by rebound lows.

Encourage your children to read. If you read to your very young child, help him to begin reading on his own, and fill your home with healthy books and magazines; your child can learn anything he wants to learn and will find a joyful avenue of imagination. Your child should be a regular visitor to both school and public libraries.

Build a support group of other children who spend time alone at home. If they can get together and talk about their fears, share how they solve problems, think of things they can do to keep from being bored or feeling alone—all problems that latchkey children face—they will develop security in knowing there are others who live the same way they do. Sometimes schools or churches can offer this kind of support group help.

If your home-alone child is a teenager who is just now experiencing being left home alone, he may not have learned how to conduct himself when no one else is around.

Take time and make opportunities to talk with your child (not just to him). Talk about his friends, what he does when he's alone at home, his chores, how he gets along with younger siblings he may be responsible for, peer pressure, drugs, alcohol, gangs, anything you can remember that concerned you when you were his age. Listen to him. Listen to her. Hear what your teenager is saying— or not saying.

Give your teenager an opportunity to discuss the house rules he feels are unfair.

Participate in as many school activities as possible to show your interest and support in his life away from home.

Further Help for Parents of Very Young Children

In an article in *Newsweek*, Dr. T. Berry Brazelton, one of America's leading pediatricians, outlined several problems working parents encounter with their babies and preschool children and suggested ways to alleviate these problems. Some of these suggestions are also helpful to parents of school-age children.

Separation: Most parents have experienced little games children play on busy school mornings. They drag their feet getting dressed, dawdle over breakfast, misplace or lose homework, and generally waste time. These are more than likely ploys children contrive to delay being separated from their working parents. When you realize this you can be more patient with your anxious children. Dr. Brazelton suggests that the family get up earlier so that there is more time to talk together, choose the right things to wear, eat a good breakfast in peace, and generally feel good about starting a new day.

Discipline: Children need the security of boundaries. One parent told her teenage children that if they were ever coerced by their peers to do something they knew was wrong, they could use her as their excuse. "My mom would kill me if I did something like that" is a good excuse that sometimes works when other kids put pressure on. Knowing their parents love them enough to be concerned about what they do, where they go, and who they see is comforting to children.

Dr. Brazelton points out that disciplines should be seen as teaching, not punishment. Parents should decide ahead of time what the rules are and stick by them. A parent who vacillates creates confusion and insecurity in a child. "Discipline should be seen as teaching rather than punishment. . . . No discipline works magically," he says. "Every episode is an opportunity to teach—but to teach over time."[5]

Sleep Issues: Bedtime for children is generally a rough time for families. Being separated from their families for long periods during the day is so painful that children sometimes fear being separated from them at night. Children will use any excuse to keep from going to their own beds: "I'm still hungry." "I have to go to the bathroom." "I forgot to tell you something." "Tell me another story." "I wanna drink." They may go to bed angry and tearful and wake up frequently during the night. These may all be symptoms of insecurity and a deep fear of being left alone.

Dr. Brazelton suggests that a "comfort object" such as a stuffed toy, favorite blanket, or other "lovey," can help children cope with separation. If your child awakens during the night, wait a few minutes to see if she settles down again by herself. If not, go in and help her find her own comfort pattern, then leave her alone again. Bedtime rituals should be established early and maintained pretty religiously.

Feeding: Establishing healthy eating habits in children is one of the most difficult jobs parents have, yet we are told that improper nutrition is responsible for all kinds of problems in children. Usually, children leave the house in the mornings with little or no food in their stomachs, yet nutritionists tell us that breakfast is the most important meal in the day. Then children who come home after school starved to death will grab sweets and other junk food to fill up on. Parents realize this and try to make the evening meal the nutritional in-loading time.

Force-feeding does little to instill a desire for healthy food in a child. Dr. Brazelton feels that an inordinate amount of time and attention are given over to the subject of food. Parents take away their children's autonomy when they work so hard to get food down stubborn little mouths. The family evening meal can be spoiled by emphasizing food rather than sharing the experiences of the day. He says, "Your relationship is more important than the quantities of food consumed."[6]

How, then, can you be sure your child is getting proper nutrition each day? Keeping food such as milk, whole-grain breads, low-fat cheese, fruits, liked vegetables, and peanut butter in the house will give a child a good choice of healthy food. Dr. Brazelton also suggests that children should take vitamin supplements.

Other advice Dr. Brazelton gives is to:

Find other people to share your family stress, such as professional, peer, or family resource groups.

Give up the idea that you can be Supermom or Superdad. No one is a perfect parent, not even that parent who spends a great deal of time with the children.

Conserve energy in the workplace so that you can have more later to give your child in the evenings.

Investigate after-school day care or other supervised activities. See about shared-job options and flexible time arrangements your company may offer.

Expect children to "fall apart" when you walk into the house. They have saved up their strongest feelings and fears for this very moment. Gather the family together when you get home. Sit close together and air all the pressing problems with patience and concern. Scolding, blaming, screaming, and feeling guilty are not ways to solve these predictable reactions, and never say, "What did you do to provoke the situation. . . ."

Set aside a special time to be with each child alone every week. Make an appointment with him. This way he will feel that he is as important to you as any other activity or person.

Don't allow yourself to become overwhelmed by stress. Work as a team with your spouse and children in solving problems. Divide the work of maintaining a family between husband and wife when possible.

Share the family chores together.[7] The old saying "many hands make light work" is still true. Telling a child to "clean up his room" means little to most children because they have no idea what your idea of a clean room is. But helping, showing, sharing, and creating a "Clean Room Checklist," which makes room cleaning a joint effort, will produce results and keep the peace. Eventually, your child will recognize a messy room and be able to clean up by himself.

What Works

It's scary to go home to an empty house and be alone even for an hour. TV becomes our only companion. Avoid creating latchkey kids at all costs. We'd rather have day care than be a latchkey kid. But, if there's no other choice:

1. Help us find friends' homes we can go to.

2. Investigate the neighborhood for friendly neighbors that will check in on us.

3. Get other moms to pool resources—a "carepool."

4. Take a late or early lunch break so that you can spend time with us. Take us to lunch on your lunch break.

5. Set rules for us to follow when we're home alone. We need to know what to do and what's expected of us: Leave a list of options rather than a list of chores. Give us some time for free activities. Remind us of things that have to get done, such as homework.

6. When you do get home, make time for us. Have special homework time, reading time, dinnertime, etc. Don't isolate us in a room by ourselves to do our homework. Work with us. Stay up with us.

7. Always tell us where we can reach you if we need you, or tell us who else we can call.

What Doesn't Work

Don't come home and immediately need time alone. Or at least let us know that we are in your schedule for a certain time. Don't push us away. Tell us when we can have some togetherness.

3

Firearms

Weapons in the home, the school, and on the streets are providing a new challenge for parents. When weapons are easily accessible in the home, not only do they pose a serious threat to the latchkey child, they also tend to show up at school and in the community. We live in a society with a penchant for solving problems in violent ways. Our children need special skills in dealing with weapons.

Gun control is one of the most controversial subjects in America. Proponents claim that violent crime would decrease if gun registration were mandatory. Opponents reply that the only people affected by gun control would be the innocent because criminals can always find guns. While the controversy rages, children and youth continue to die or become permanently injured from bullet wounds.

The purpose of this chapter is not to add fuel to the flames of controversy. However, judging from the many reports of injury and death as a result of guns, something should be said about parental gun control within the confines of private residences, especially where children and young people live.

One of our nation's largest public education programs published a booklet on child safety that includes every threat to the life and well-being of our nation's children except one: firearms. The sixteen-page booklet published by the National Safe Kids Campaign, a program of Washington, D.C.'s Children's Hospital National Medical Center and supported by Johnson & Johnson, AMOCO, and the National Safety Council, includes danger from traffic accidents, drownings, burns, poisoning, choking, and falls as primary causes of injury among children. The booklet claims that no type of unintentional injury to America's youth has been excluded, yet it contains nothing about injury or death by firearms.[1] Statistics, however, indicate that firearms are a very real threat to child safety.

How can you ensure that your children will be *safety-smart* about firearms? Four ways: (1) Consider and believe the facts about the danger of firearms. (2) If you have guns in your home, thoroughly educate your children about their danger. (3) Help your children protect themselves if they are in a place where there are guns. (4) Realize that BB guns and air guns are often as dangerous as other types of firearms.

Consider the Facts

- A State of Washington study indicated that friends, acquaintances, or relatives were killed by home guns twelve times more frequently than strangers.

- Each year, from 1,500 to 3,400 youths commit suicide with firearms.

- One thousand handgun murder victims each year are under nineteen years old. Nearly three-hundred more are killed by other types of firearms. Of the total fatalities, 279 are fifteen years old or younger.

- Of the four hundred children killed by firearms every year, forty are children under five years of age.[2]

- In Los Angeles County in 1991 at least eight thousand people were hit by bullets—almost one an hour.[3]

Some families keep guns for seemingly legitimate reasons. Scott, age ten, was "just playing" with his dad's .357 magnum. His detective dad kept the gun loaded in the event some punk he had arrested decided to even the score. It was the biggest gun young Scott had ever seen. As he handled the firearm with awe he felt great pride in his dad. Scott loved the stories on TV of being a cop on the street and he ached for the day he could wear a badge and carry a gun just like Dad. Scott jabbed the gun into an imaginary holster in his belt. He heard an explosion as the gun kicked out of his hand. But that's all he remembered. He passed out from pain. Luckily, a neighbor heard the shot and Scott's scream. When the boy awoke in the hospital his right foot was in a cast; the front half was missing. His dream of being a policeman ended in one split second.[4]

In another incident, Paul and his friend Andy, both twelve, were playing cops and robbers. Paul knew that his dad, a prison psychologist whose life had been threatened by inmates a number of times, kept a shotgun in the upstairs closet "just in case." Paul, however, did not realize that the gun was kept loaded. The boy ran to the closet, grabbed the gun and pointed it at his friend, not really aiming and not intending to shoot. The gun went off and flew out of his hands. Paul watched in horror as Andy slammed backward against the wall as though yanked by some incredible invisible force. Blood flew everywhere. In just a second Paul's friend lay dead.[5]

A CBS television special on July 5, 1991, told about an Orlando, Florida, youth who accidentally shot his best friend in the face while showing off a gun. The incident occurred soon after a new law had been passed that held parents responsible for any accidental shooting involving children. The youth's father, a career Navy man, kept a gun on a shelf in his closet. At his trial he claimed the gun was always left unloaded and was at a loss to explain how an "unloaded" gun could have fired. The family engaged a private detective to look into the matter. In questioning the youth, the detective asked him if he had ever played with the gun prior to the accident. The boy admitted that a week or ten days earlier he had taken the gun, found an ammunition clip, and put it in the gun. After playing with it a while he placed the weapon back on the shelf. However, he did not remember taking out the clip.

Because the new law held parents answerable for accidents involving children and firearms, the father was found guilty of not seeing that the weapon was secure. The jury's responsibility was to determine if he was guilty of gross neglect, a felony which would result in a jail sentence and the loss of his Navy pension, or guilty of leaving a loaded gun where a child could get at it, a misdemeanor. The jury ruled that he was guilty of a misdemeanor. He received six months' probation and paid a fine of five hundred dollars and an undisclosed amount to the injured boy and his family.

The injured boy is now blind in one eye as a result of the accident; the relationship between the two families has been seriously damaged, and doubt remains in many minds about the jury's verdict. The two boys are still the best of friends. All this grief could have been avoided by properly educating both youths on the extreme danger of firearms.[6]

If You Have Guns in Your Home . . .

The kind of personal and family gun control you need to establish within your home may be determined by where you live. Children who live in rural areas generally become familiar with guns when they are very young. They are taken hunting with their families, taught to shoot predators that raid the henhouse, given instructions on how to clean, load, unload, store, and carry firearms.

Children who live in the inner city also become familiar with guns, many times out of necessity. They learn from older siblings how to protect themselves from violent gang members, drug dealers, robbers, and abusers and how to assert themselves in life-threatening environments. However people learn about them, the indiscriminate use of firearms can kill and maim. People who own guns need to exercise some kind of control over their use or abuse.

The *Journal of the American Medical Association* listed several accidents associated with the perceived need for protection. In one case a five-year- old boy found a loaded .38 revolver under an older family member's pillow. The gun was usually stored six feet above the floor, out of sight, but was put under the pillow at night. When the older family member left the bedroom for a few minutes to watch television, the five-year- old found the gun and shot himself in the head.

Another incident tells about an eleven-year- old boy who was shot in the head by his twelve-year- old brother with a twelve-gauge shotgun. Ordinarily, the gun was kept unloaded. The previous night, however, the father had loaded the gun when he saw a prowler. He neglected to unload it in the morning, and the boys began to play with the gun, not knowing it was loaded.[7]

These are samples of stories that are told almost daily in newspapers across the country of accidental shootings with guns kept for self-defense.

If there is a firearm in a home, parents should explain why it is there and discuss gun ownership with their children. Every member of the family should be taught—preferably by professional teachers—how to safely handle, use, maintain, and store firearms.

The National Rifle Association (NRA), well-known for its support of gun ownership and its stand against gun control, provides information and education to the general public about safe gun use. One leaflet says:

> There is no perfect age to talk with your child about gun safety. . . . A good time to introduce gun safety is when your child starts acting out "gun play" or asks questions. . . . Children see guns on TV and in the movies. This is entertainment. Make sure your child understands the difference between pretend and real life. Actors on television use play guns. They pretend to be wounded and to die. After the show, they get up and appear in other films or on other TV stations. Don't assume that your child knows that. Explain it. Make certain your child knows the difference between a toy gun and a real gun. . . . Guns such as BB guns and firearms—pistols, rifles, and shotguns—are not toys.
>
> Gun safety is common sense. Always point the gun in a safe direction—either upward or toward the ground. Keep your finger off the trigger. When handling a gun there is a natural tendency to put your finger on the trigger. Don't do it!! Keep the gun unloaded. . . . If you do not know how to

check to see if a gun is unloaded, leave it alone and get help from someone who does know. Many accidents occur because someone thought a gun was not loaded. Keep all guns unloaded until ready to use. . . . If you own a gun . . . it is your responsibility to set a positive example for your child.[8]

It is not known how much such education has reduced the incidence of injury and death by gunshot. However, if you have guns in your home and feel you are justified in owning them and storing them there, then you are responsible for the consequences of your decision.

One man whose life was permanently altered by a firearm shared this story:

It was quite a piece of machinery, all right—heavy, smooth, lightly oiled, and deadly. It was a double action revolver—a .38 caliber Smith and Wesson Police Special. My grandfather had carried it for all his street years as a Philadelphia cop. He had never drawn it in the line of duty. Now the gun was my father's. It was kept in its holster in the back of the locked top drawer of a chiffonier in my parents' bedroom. I'd never seen it until this day, when my father took it out to clean and oil it.

He had never fired it. I was ten years old, and mightily impressed by its heft and its action—the cylinder revolving to exactly the right chamber space when the hammer was cocked or even when the trigger was pulled. My father let me handle it and snap the trigger a few times. It made a satisfying and final clack as it fell. Then he took it away, warned me about touching it, and locked it up.

A few days later this ten-year-old had some friends over and decided to show off a little. He had already figured out a way to get into the locked drawer and had taken the gun out and practiced a few fancy draws in front of a mirror. This day he ran through the house waving the gun at his friends and shouting "pakow!" All the kids, except his friend Jackie, ran down the stairs to the cellar. Jackie stopped at the top of the stairs and turned to say something.

The gun-toter raised the .38 and pulled the trigger just as he had several times before. This time, however, there was no satisfying "clack" but rather an ear-shattering roar like a bomb exploding. The bullet tore into Jackie's face and passed through his brain, tearing a huge chunk out of the back of his skull.

The storyteller's life changed from then on. The kids at school avoided him and teachers probed him with subtle questions, trying to find out more details. He changed schools but the stories followed him until he graduated from high school. But he learned something from the terrible experience. He learned the dreadful power of a handgun, "a power for which no western pulp stories, no comic books, no cowboy movies, no radio programs had ever prepared me."

Even though he went into the service and became a qualified marksman with a .45 pistol and an expert marksman with a carbine, he now looks upon handguns as he does rattlesnakes: "handsome, beautifully made, and fascinating—but at the same time repulsive and full of deadly menace. When I think of the number of handguns kept for 'protection' in American homes—thirty million at the last conservative estimate—I think of thirty million rattlesnakes coiled and ready to strike. For I know that the odds are overwhelmingly great that any one of those guns that is fired will kill or wound a child, a spouse, a family member, or a friend."[9]

If you keep guns in your home because you feel a need to defend yourself and your family, you should know that your gun could become the means of injury or death to you or another family member. Many people can testify that a gun did not protect them when they came face-to-face with an intruder. Ordinary people hesitate to shoot another person, regardless of the circumstances. Professional robbers, gang members, and narcotics addicts do not have this hesitancy. The shoot-out, in these cases, becomes terribly one-sided with the inexperienced, non-violent homeowner becoming the victim. Perhaps you and your family could consider alternate methods of protecting yourselves and your possessions.

Whether or not you keep firearms in the house, all family members should practice "emergency intruder drills" so that each one will know what to do if an intruder enters your house, just as they learn how to respond in case of fire.

If Someone Displays a Gun Where You Are

Even if you do not keep firearms in your home, your children can become threatened by them. More and more children are carrying weapons to school—sometimes as a lark, sometimes as a defense against other students, sometimes as a means of getting their own way, sometimes with premeditated intent to shoot someone. These weapons are in fact often used—accidentally or deliberately.

Some American schools are adding curriculum that deals with guns and other weapons. These teaching sessions begin in preschool classes and continue throughout high school. Teachers of very young children (preschool through fifth grades) may read picture storybooks such as *The Butter Battle Book*, where the Yooks and Zooks battle with weapons over which side of bread should be buttered, or *Dana Doesn't Like Guns Anymore*, which tells how Dana wanted a gun like his friends had. When he accidentally shoots his bird friend with a borrowed BB gun, he no longer likes guns.

The NRA has a "Dick and Jane" color booklet for very young children that emphasizes three rules: "If a child finds a gun, he or she should follow these basic safety measures: Stop – Don't Touch. Leave the Area. Tell an Adult."[10]

Children in the classroom may role-play a scenario in which several of them try to talk a friend out of playing with a gun. They learn the pledge, "If I ever see a gun, or anything that looks like a gun, or part of a gun, I won't touch it. I'll go and tell an adult because guns can hurt me."

Sixth- to twelfth-grade students watch videos about teenagers and their families who were victims of gun violence. They talk about anger and how to control it, express it, and channel it. Teachers emphasize: "Guns kill! Don't mess with them and don't hang out with people who do!"

While weapon control at school is primarily the responsibility of school authorities, your children may be threatened by firearms in other places. In our gun-conscious nation, children can encounter someone with a gun almost anywhere they go—school, the store, the park, in the streets, and in their friends' homes. In addition to instructing your elementary school child, "Only stay one hour at Tommy's house," and, "If you go somewhere else, call me and tell me," parents may have to say, "And if Tommy pulls a gun on you, come home immediately." If the parents of your child's friends have acted responsibly, you will not have to worry too much about your son or daughter being threatened or tantalized by a firearm. But if the parents are not so responsible, your child may be in danger at their home.

We will never rid our country of firearms. We have to learn to live with them. That means we have to educate our children about their potential danger.

BB Guns, Air Guns, and Look-Alike Guns

Helen Orsette tours Michigan and Washington, D.C., trying to force manufacturers and the Consumer Product Safety Commission to strictly regulate the sale of BB guns and air rifles. On August 15, 1988, her two-year-old son Joey was playing in an upstairs bedroom with his ten-year-old stepbrother Tony. Tony found a "toy gun" and shot several blasts of air. Thinking it was harmless, he pointed it around the room while jumping on the bed. The movement of jumping on the bed must have dislodged a BB that was hidden in the chamber. A BB struck Joey in the chest, traveled between his ribs and into his heart, killing him. The gun belonged to another son, age eighteen, who had stored it on an upstairs shelf when he left for the Navy.

Mrs. Orsette's personal investigation showed that BB guns of today are not the ones she grew up with. The power and velocity of these guns now equal that of a "real" gun.[11] Injuries from gas/air or spring- operated guns requiring hospital emergency room treatment average about 21,000 a year. Sixty percent of those occur in the five- to fourteen-year age group.[12] Some air guns are capable of reaching lethal levels.

Parents of kids who are *safety-smart* will take precautions with guns. They will see to it that:

- Guns are stored away *unloaded* and locked in tamperproof containers with the keys put safely away.

- Ammunition is locked up *separately*.

- Their children are warned and educated about the extreme danger of firearms— of all kinds.

- If their children are allowed to use guns, they will give them complete instructions about their use, including the warning that the guns are to be used only when a parent is around.

- They do not give their children a "toy" air rifle or BB gun

- They will answer their children's questions about guns openly and honestly and not make a gun an object of curiosity.

Look-alike guns pose another threat for the child who may decide to use them in a public setting where a law enforcement officer may confuse them for real weapons and inadvertently place the child in harm's way.

What Works

1. Teach us gun safety from the time we first begin to play with toy guns.

2. Talk with us about movies and TV shows that include gun violence.

3. Show us articles in the newspaper about gun accidents.

4. Teach us to stay away from people with guns, even friends.

5. Give us something more fascinating than guns—laser tag, sports, and karate all offer forms of self-protection.

6. Role-play with us what we should do when we encounter someone with a gun, like the commercial where a man says to a kid, "Take these drugs. The first one is free." And the kid says, "No, no." And the man turns out to be the dad and says, "Good job, Son, that's exactly what you're supposed to do."

What Doesn't Work

Ignoring guns. Pretending that they don't exist. Even if our family doesn't have guns we will all eventually encounter them somewhere. We need to know what to do when we do.

4

Alcohol

Most parents know better than to leave toxic substances around where young children can get them. They carefully put poisonous cleaning supplies in high cupboards, cover paint cans, and keep childproof lids on aspirin and other medications. Yet in their refrigerators are six-packs of beer, and liquor cabinets display bottles of gin, whisky, bourbon, scotch, and vodka. Even if these substances are not found in your home, they could be in the homes of your children's friends. Therefore, your children need to be educated about the poisonous drug, alcohol.

The National Council on Alcoholism estimates that of the nine million alcoholics in the United States only 3 percent are found on skid row. The other 97 percent are still in homes, offices, schools, and factories—despite their dependency.[1]

Alcohol is particularly dangerous to children and teenagers. Children do not start out intending to get addicted to alcohol; they honestly believe it could never happen to them. If they did, most of them would never start to drink.

Although the media give much attention to illegal drugs such as marijuana and cocaine, the illegal drug used most by children under twenty-one is alcohol.[2] Also, the only negative mention of alcohol in the media concerns drinking and driving. Let's look at some facts about the use of alcohol among children and teens.

- By age eighteen a child will have seen seventy-five thousand drinking scenes on television, presented in such a way as to make alcohol seem harmless, acceptable, fun, and desirable.[3]

- A 1989 University of Michigan survey among high school seniors indicated that 60 percent had drunk alcohol in the last month, 33 percent had five or more drinks in a row within the previous two weeks, and 4.2 percent drank every day. Other surveys indicate that 40 percent of sixth-graders have tasted wine coolers and a total of 95 percent of high school seniors drink.[4]

- Out of twenty-two thousand deaths due to drinking and driving in 1990, 2,775 were teens. Even though teens account for only 17 percent of this country's licensed drivers, they are responsible for 36 percent of all fatal drunk driving accidents.[5]

- Studies show that a quarter of all hospitalized patients have alcohol-related problems. Children who use alcohol at a young age are more likely to increase alcohol use as they mature and to experience by late adolescence alcohol-related problems that affect their health, their relationships, and their home lives. They are more likely to do poorly in school, get into trouble with authorities, and become more sexually permissive.[6]

Alcohol Addiction: A Problem in Children

Most people who become addicted to alcohol begin drinking in their own homes. Claire Costales, author of several books on overcoming alcoholism, says: "I was on my way to becoming an alcoholic the first time I took a drink. I was quite young when that happened—as best I can remember, about ten years old when I was first permitted to have a cup of Christmas nog. Before that, I was allowed to take sips of my parents' drinks. But this was not considered 'drinking' you understand. Just innocent sips."[7] Claire got her first taste of what eventually brought her down in her own home.

A mother of a sixteen-year-old boy wrote to "Dear Abby" asking her to settle a dispute between her and her husband. Their son, his girlfriend, and three other couples were planning to rent a hotel room for their post-prom party so they could drink beer. The mother thought that since the kids "were going to drink anyway," it would be better for them to have the party in her home for three reasons: They would not have to worry about their son being out in his car and drinking because she could hold all the car keys; they lived only five miles from the school where the prom was being held; it would not cost the parents anything because the kids would pay for their own beer and snacks and she could give them coffee in the morning before they left her home. She felt this was a sensible solution to a potentially dangerous situation. The lady said the only problem with her idea was her husband. He went nuts! He felt that his wife was encouraging the kids to drink.

Abby's answer was to vote with the husband because, first, the plan condoned teenage drinking and, second, permitting minors to drink alcohol is against the law. She suggested that the woman host the party in her home and provide food, soft drinks— *and* supervision.[8]

Reasoning that kids are "going to drink anyway" is the same as letting them play with a loaded gun. Children and youths are not physically or emotionally equipped to handle a drug as powerful as alcohol. Some will *never* be able to handle alcohol because they are among those who are psychologically or physically predisposed to alcoholism.

Most teenagers are able to get hold of alcohol even if there is none in their homes, and they are often tempted by peer pressure to try it. Parents should realize that some young people who experiment with alcohol never progress into alcoholism. They do not live long enough.

Gene, age thirteen, had watched his dad drink at home all his life. Sometimes his dad would brag that a "real man" could "belt 'em down and hold 'em like a man." One day after school, Gene and his friend were alone in Gene's house, feeling like doing something manly. They went to Dad's liquor cabinet and challenged each other to see who could drink—like a man—the most the fastest and not show any effects. They chose vodka because they'd heard it didn't leave an after-odor, mixing it with Coke to make it more palatable. After drinking about half a pint they didn't feel a thing, so they started guzzling the liquid fire right out of the bottle—"like real men."

After finishing the first pint, they broke open the second. Gene raised the bottle to his lips, accustomed by now to the sting, and poured as much as he could into his mouth. His eyes brimmed with tears, his throat blazed, but he only winced a little as he fought back the urge to spit it all out. Very quickly the room started to spin and he began to retch. He passed out. His frightened friend had sense enough to call for help, but by the time Gene arrived at the hospital his vital signs spelled real trouble. Before the doctors could complete emergency procedures, Gene died. Diagnosis: Alcohol poisoning through overdose; blood alcohol level .50. But thirteen-year-old Gene proved he was a "real man."[9]

Michelle was a straight-A student all through school. She was valedictorian at her graduation and was deluged with scholarship offers from top universities. She chose a four-year, all-tuition-paid ride at Stanford. Her future was set. She was riding high. She deserved it. She was a winner.

Michelle went to a beach party for student leaders and high-GPA students. None of these kids were losers. There was beer at the party, but no one got drunk. These kids had brains and they were careful. Michelle didn't touch a drink, and the young man Michelle was dating had only a few beers, but he was not aware of what even small amounts of alcohol can do to one's perception and coordination. When he was driving Michelle home after the party in the early morning darkness, he approached a flatbed truck a little too fast. He miscalculated the distance and hit his brakes too late. The car slid under the truck's bed, slicing off the top of the car. Michelle and her date were instantly decapitated.[10]

Granted, these are extreme examples, but they are not as rare as you would like to think. How can you help protect your child from the dangers associated with drinking alcohol?

Educating Your Children About Alcohol Danger

According to many educators, alcoholism is the top substance abuse problem in schools today.[11] Many children start using alcohol before junior high.[12] Some schools, in cooperation with law enforcement agencies, present programs that educate kids about drugs, including alcohol. But the lessons lose their punch if they are not reinforced by parents. And the lessons must begin while the children are young because young children are more susceptible to alcohol addiction than adults are. The typical adult may take four to six years of persistent drinking to become an alcoholic. The juvenile can become one much faster, within six months in some cases.[13]

In an article entitled "Substance Abuse," Loretta Middleton and Christine Campbell, who helped develop child safety curriculum standards for the National School Safety Center, address ways that parents and school authorities can help children and young people become aware of the dangers of alcohol use. They say that alcohol is a drug that can devastate the psychological, physiological, intellectual, and social lives of youth and their families. Their purpose in writing is to reach students before they have a chance to try alcohol or drugs.

The two authors give several "standards" that children at each grade level should be taught that will prepare them to reject alcohol experimentation. Children from kindergarten through sixth grade need to "understand how their feelings and attitudes affect their actions." "They should be aware of their unique personal strengths."

Young people, grades seven through twelve need to know that they are "responsible for maintaining a healthy body and mind." They need to know the negative effects of alcohol, the stages of alcohol dependency, appropriate and healthy ways of expressing and dealing with feelings and stress. They should understand how peers and families influence their personal values. They should see that advertising, TV, and movies affect decision-making. Finally, they should know that using alcohol is illegal for them, even though it is considered a legal drug, and that they will suffer the consequences—both personally and legally—if they use it.[14]

Help your child understand how his feelings and attitudes affect his actions. Sometimes children turn to chemical abuse to deal with life and stress. They are confused about their feelings and do not know how to handle them. Children should understand that feelings are normal. It is okay to be happy, sad, angry, and frightened. Everyone has these feelings. They should be guided in expressing their feelings verbally to parents, teachers, or their friends. They do this by using "I" statements: "I feel happy today because . . ." or "I feel sad today because. . . ." Parents, praise your child when he honestly shares why he feels happy or sad. Assure him that everyone has these feelings, that they do not require some reaction. This way he will grow up being able to vent frustrations and fears and not hold them inside until they build to the point where alcohol or drugs appear to be the only solution.

Help your child know her own unique personal strengths. Many young people give in to peer pressure to drink because they have poor self-esteem and little confidence. Children should be helped to think positively. If your daughter finds fault with the way she looks, help her see a special quality about herself that is attractive and appealing to other children. Praise her each day for at least one positive thing she does. It may seem small and insignificant to you, but it can be very encouraging to your child. This can be extended by suggesting that your daughter tell what she likes about her younger or older brother or sister or friend. When you or anyone else compliments your daughter, teach her to accept the compliment by saying "Thank you" without discounting or qualifying it.

On an especially bad day help your son list things he likes about himself. Help him to think of personality and character traits as well as physical attributes. Then have him mount the list on the bathroom mirror or in his room so that he can look at it every day.

Teach your children to set goals that are achievable. Then help them celebrate each time they reach a goal.

Teach them that they are responsible for maintaining their own healthy bodies and minds. Many times a child will begin to drink or take drugs because he honestly does not believe he is lovable or worthwhile. Therefore, he does not think it is worth the effort to treat himself well. Encourage your child to ask for a hug when he needs to feel acceptable or be comforted.

Know how to deal with your child's maturing emotions and stress. Often teens have trouble expressing themselves to their parents. They need to know who they can talk to and where they can find help in times of crisis. Talk about the things that create good mental health. Discuss how being exposed to negative influences can affect thought patterns. Such things as a steady diet of gory horror films will not lead to healthy minds.

Help your child to talk about things he sees and hears. Encourage him to ask questions about things he does not understand or fears. Explain how we often fear things that are perhaps not frightening, or how we become overly sensitive to "problems" that can actually become "challenges" when we see them in a different light.

Understand how peer groups and your own family can influence personal values. Talk about peer pressure with your kids. All children want to be accepted by their peers. A wise parent will help a child accept herself the way she is and realize that it is okay to be different from other kids. Sometimes we assume that others don't like us when we are actually pushing them away because we cannot accept ourselves. Teaching children at an early age what is clearly right and what is just as clearly wrong is a great help when they have to make hard decisions about following the crowd. An earnest religious upbringing often sustains kids when peer pressure becomes heavy.

Be aware of the great impact advertising, TV, and movies have on decision-making. Explain how advertising can distort what is real. Kids are exposed to much media advertising, most of which depicts a false picture of what is healthy. Watch commercials on television with your kids and comment on the distorted view these commercials show. Explain that advertisers will use *any* means honest or otherwise to sell their products, even if the end result is death and destruction.

Listen to the music your kids play. Rather than being judgmental about the music itself, explain how some of the lyrics present a false and unhealthy picture of healthy and safe living.

Team up with school teachers in discouraging alcohol use. The people who are responsible for teaching your children reading, writing, and arithmetic cannot cover all the bases in your child's life. Teachers and school administrators need your support, cooperation, and input. Get to know the people who work with your kids for a major part of every weekday. Teachers and parents together can make a big difference in how children perceive the damaging influences they encounter every day.

What Alcohol Does to Your Body

What is wrong with drinking alcohol, especially for children and young people? For one thing, it's illegal. But because alcohol is so readily available to almost anyone, they think it is socially acceptable to drink. Kids see their parents, teachers, and friends drink. They see apparently healthy and attractive people drink in movies, on television, and in real life. Their sports heroes guzzle and advertise beer. Extensive exposure to the acceptability of drinking alcohol leads children to believe there is nothing wrong with this drug. However, many are not able to control this very powerful yet subtle drug.

Alcohol depresses the central nervous system. It easily enters the brain and impairs judgment and behavior. One drink may cause the person to become more lively, talkative (not necessarily sensible talk, however), slightly flushed, sometimes goofy, and often drowsy and lethargic. Alcohol acts on your brain by making parts, the inhibitory parts, less active. It alters your judgment and changes the way you act and feel.

Large doses of alcohol, especially in children and youths, can cause unconsciousness and death. Death occurs when the central nervous system is depressed to the point that breathing and other vital processes cease.

Some people like to drink because alcohol makes them less inhibited. They believe they are more clever, cool, and attractive when they drink. Some people drink because alcohol helps them blot out pain and unpleasantness in their lives. But when the stupor ends, the unpleasantness is still there. A great many people become so dependent on alcohol that it becomes their master. They no longer have control of their own lives.

There is no difference between the alcohol in beer and the alcohol in whisky. A twelve - ounce bottle of beer, a four - ounce glass of wine, and one-and-one-half ounces of whisky, gin, or vodka, straight or mixed with soda or juice, all contain the same amount of alcohol.[15]

Most parents nag or threaten their children about drinking and taking care of their bodies, but sometimes it is more helpful to use visual aids. Show pictures that illustrate what alcohol does to a liver. Reinforce what schools teach about nutrition, exercise, and sleeping habits.

Inasmuch as you cannot be with your child every minute of every day to monitor what influences him, he is going to have to assume much of the responsibility for his own health and well-being. Children should understand the consequences of alcohol consumption and be encouraged to take responsibility for their own actions. If you drink alcohol, however, it is difficult to explain to your son why he is not allowed to emulate your practice. Explain that he must wait until he is of legal age and physically and emotionally mature. The illegal use of legal substances is wrong and harmful and can be fatal.

What Works

1. We don't drink because we're Christians. We want to show people that we mean what we profess. The minute

someone sees you with a beer he assumes that you're a drinker. We don't want that reputation. Adults can have a beer or wine with dinner and not be labeled "drinkers"; it's not like that with teenagers. It's black and white with teens, not gray.

2. Show that you trust us. It's probably better to keep us from going to parties where there will be alcohol, but if we go, let us know that you are deeply concerned. Talk to us about it. Find out where we'll be and tell us to call if we change locations, need a ride home, or feel it's time to leave the party.

3. Make us responsible. When you say, "You can go to the party as long as *you* drive," it gives us the feeling that we are trusted, so we act trustworthy. This also gives us an excuse not to drink. We can responsibly and maturely say, "No, I'm the designated driver."

4. Help us choose the right friends when we are young. This way we learn to develop healthy relationships later. When our friends don't drink, we don't feel pressured to drink.

5. You taught us when we were young that we don't need or want to drink. We knew that if we started we might not be able to quit. You were an example for us. You seldom drank in our home.

6. Tell us that we can be taken advantage of when we've had something to drink. Also tell us that it makes us fat!

What Doesn't Work

Telling us to do what you say and not what you do.

PART II

Safe
in
the
Classroom

5

Bullies

R ight to Safe Schools. All students and staff of primary, elementary, junior high and senior high schools have the inalienable right to attend campuses which are safe, secure and peaceful." This statement in the California Constitution reflects the feelings of every parent in America.[1] Developing the skills for success—reading, writing, thinking, evaluating, and decision-making—are all important. However, teachers cannot teach and students cannot learn in an environment of danger, intimidation, and fear. Ensuring "safe schools" is a parental responsibility shared with a variety of school, community, and youth-serving professionals. If we are going to require children to attend school, then we must provide an environment that is safe, secure, and peaceful.

While some schools in the United States do not have some of the more extreme problems discussed in Part II, every school has bullies.

Just one month before school let out for the summer, eight-year-old Leslie started crying every time her mother stopped the car to let her and her brother and sister out in front of the school. Leslie's mother thought the child was just getting tired of school or being stubborn.

This was their first year at the new school. Fourteen-year-old Jonathan, eleven-year-old Michelle, and Leslie had gone to the same school in their old neighborhood since kindergarten. But when their parents divorced and their mother moved out of the school district, they began to attend the new school where they were not known. Michelle and Jonathan adapted rather quickly, but Leslie missed her old friends and teachers in the other smaller school.

As it turned out, the family moved back into the old school district the next year. Jonathan went on to high school, Leslie and Michelle went back to their old school. A year and a half later, Leslie told her mother why she had hated the other school: Some older boys would wait for her to come onto the school ground. They would chase her, hit her, and generally make life miserable. She was a victim of childhood bullying. Having been taught not to tattle, Leslie would not tell her teacher or her mother what was happening. She just built up a fear and hatred of school.[2]

Tommy, twelve, is taller and heavier than the other children in his sixth-grade class, and has a mild nature. His parents took him out of a small private school and enrolled him in a public school with classrooms three times the size of the ones he had been used to because they thought it would be good for him to have a wider range of friends and experiences. Not only is Tommy bigger than his classmates, he is slightly dyslexic.

In less than a month, Tommy's parents could see that their son was very unhappy. After much probing they got him to admit that his classmates—both boys and girls—made life miserable for him, calling him "fatso" and "dummy," and refused to associate with him. His parents put him back into the small school where everyone knew and accepted him.[3]

These two incidents represent the bullying and intimidation that invade too many of our schools and communities. "Bullying is perhaps the most enduring and underrated problem in our schools today," say Stuart Greenbaum, Brenda Turner, and Ronald D. Stephens. "The problem of bullying has existed for as long as children have been going to school. In fact, most adults remember their school-yard bully—often by name."[4] Despite the immediate and long-term effects, most American schools have yet to address ways to combat the problem.

Tolerating bullies fuels every other aspect of school and community crime. Nearly three million incidents of crime and violence are reported in public schools each year, according to the National Crime Survey conducted by the U.S. Bureau of the Census.[5] This means that about 16,000 criminal incidents per school day are *reported*– or one every six seconds. Many other such demonstrations go unreported because teachers and students fear retaliation. These incidents are not just simple acts of intimidation; rather they are criminal perpetrations—robbery, aggravated assault, and violent victimization. The reports generally track only physical losses or damage, never the psychological or emotional harm.

About one in seven of all school children becomes involved in either bullying or being bullied. One in ten students becomes a victim to some degree. Younger students are more often victimized, twice as many in grades two to six as in higher grades. More than 50 percent said they were victims of older students. These startling statistics came out of recent studies conducted in the United States, Norway, Australia, Finland, Poland, and Israel[6] –all countries with similar school systems. Bullies create a climate of fear and anxiety. Such an environment, of course, diminishes the learning process.

A "bully" is a person who inflicts physical, verbal, or emotional abuse. Bullying may involve name-calling, ethnic slurs, teasing, embarrassing, hitting, shoving, chasing, threatening, intimidating, excluding, or ostracizing. Bullying can evolve into petty theft, extortion of lunch money, harsh pranks, or imposing "territorial" bans, and graduate into assault, sexual molestation and assault, stabbing, or shooting. Whatever the conflict, the potential for violence is present. If the problem is ignored, both bully and victim suffer.

What can you do if you suspect that your child is a victim of a bully, or if you see evidence that your child is a bully?

The Victim of a Bully

Few children have the courage to stand up to a bully. They will put up with the harassment until classmates begin to shun them, the victims, as they usually do the underdog. Soon a tormented child feels too ashamed or afraid to admit his plight to parents or teachers. Eventually, the child may withdraw and underachieve in school or he may let his frustrations explode, as twelve-year-old Nathan Farris did. After being habitually tormented by classmates, Nathan brought a .45 caliber automatic to school one day to serve as his equalizer. When it (the equalizing) was over, both Nathan and one of his fellow students were dead.[7]

Another victim of bullies might take flight by skipping school completely (actually 8 percent of those who are truant[8]) or by playing sick. Some children truly become ill under the pressure. Others run away from home when they can think of no other way to escape their misery. In some extreme cases, the dread of school reaches the point where suicide may appear the only recourse the child can see out of a fear-filled situation.

If he decides to tough it out, he may be forced to steer clear of unsafe turf—school restrooms, unsupervised play areas, and certain routes to and from school. In the publication *School Safety*, Dr. Dan Olweus of Norway, who has researched school bullying and victimization for twenty years, describes the typical bully victim as someone who:

- is more anxious and insecure than students in general.

- is often cautious, sensitive, shy, and quiet.

- reacts by crying and withdrawing when attacked (at least, younger children do).

- does not have a positive self-view.

- thinks he is a failure, stupid, ashamed, and unattractive.

- is usually lonely and abandoned at school, not having a single good friend.

- is not aggressive.

- does not tease.

- in the case of boys, is generally physically weaker than his peers.[9] (It has also been revealed that male victims of bullies are closer to their mothers and often over-protected.[10])

The authors of *Set Straight on Bullies* give several ways that a parent can tell if a child is being bullied:

Watch for symptoms. Your child may be withdrawn, start getting lower grades, lose his appetite, not want to go to school, or come home with bruises or torn clothing. Many of these children may develop psychosomatic symptoms such as headaches and stomach pains as a response to this kind of stress. Be suspicious if your child often needs extra school supplies or extra lunch money; a bully may be extorting the things your child "loses."

Talk, but listen, too. Communicate openly, but try not to pry. Encourage your child to talk about school, the teachers, his friends, what he does before school, at recess and lunch, and about his walk or ride to and from school. Find out if he is hesitant to use the restrooms or play on the playground.[11]

If you suspect that your child is being bullied at school, there are several things you can do to stop it.

Tell someone at school. Tell the teacher or principal immediately what you suspect. Keep a written record of the times, dates, names, and circumstances of any bullying incidents. This kind of record will indicate to school officials that a pattern may be developing.

Find out what rules your school has about the way children are expected to behave. You need to know what your child's school expects of its students. How is the school protecting students from bullies?

Teach your child to be assertive—but not aggressive. Knowing how to avoid situations where push can come to shove is key in dealing with a bully. Boost your child's self-esteem. Teach all your children to respect one another's persons—our bodies and minds are the only things we truly own. Our bodies and our minds are private property; no one has a right to trespass on our property without *our* permission. That means your child does not have to tolerate being hit, called names, embarrassed, ridiculed, or otherwise demeaned in the eyes of others or in his own self-image by students at school or by members of his own family. Teach all your children when they are still very young that their bodies are their own private property.

If your child is often the brunt of teasing or bullying, inquire about programs that will boost his self-esteem and help him recognize his good and admirable qualities, make friends, socialize, and communicate with other children.

If your child is not able to discourage a bully by standing up to him verbally, he may be forced into protecting himself physically. Deep down inside, bullies, just like everyone else, hate pain—at least the receiving of it. And more than hating pain they positively hate to sport that lingering black eye, fat or split lip, or be seen with a bloodied nose. All these are signs of being bested. A bully will seldom go toe-to-toe with someone who is known to fight back, even a bad fighter.

This is not to say that you should teach your child to be aggressive. But if your child cannot avoid a situation, if the bully persists in bullying, you should see that he gets some training in self-defense to help build his self-confidence. Be aware, however, that "fighting back" often escalates the problem. Always report any bullying incident to proper adult authorities, including law enforcement agencies. Ask them how you should instruct your child to respond if there is another incident.

Inquire about peer counseling groups. Children should be taught to root for the underdog, not encourage the bully. By teaching kids constructive, peaceful, user-friendly alternatives to fighting (for handling conflicts), the peer counseling program can reduce incidents of physically aggressive conflict. Also, by placing a higher value on peaceful means of conflict resolution, a school can make bullying and the bully be perceived as not cool, and no one wants to be seen as not cool.

Bullying is wrong. Hurting another child physically or emotionally is wrong. Find out if your child is learning social skills in school. If not, encourage the school district to implement such a program, and work on the child's social skills at home.

Probably most important, *keep open communication with your child.* Talk to her about school. Find out what she likes or dislikes about the school, her teacher, and fellow students. Don't criticize her opinions, just listen. Add authors Greenbaum, Turner, and Stephens, "Invest quality time with your child. It is all too easy to drop children off at school in the first grade, then pick them up twelve years later and wonder what went wrong in between. Kids require time and attention, and they tend to reflect the care and thoughtfulness shown to them."[12]

Unfortunately, most children will not talk about being victimized to anyone—parents, teachers, or the police. Therefore, parents must take an active interest in what is happening at school. The idea that "the top banana keeps in touch with the bunch" makes a lot of sense when describing a parent's role in his child's life.

Meanwhile, at the parental end of things, when we hear of bullying going on against kids other than our own—and the key here is kids other than our own—we need to *rear up in righteous anger and defend them to our highest verbal ability.* We need to go in and have serious talks with the principal in defense of the other kid. (If the kid is our own, we risk making him look like someone who can't protect or defend himself, something we should never risk doing for his own good.) If the principal is ineffective we should repair to the superintendent's office. If he or she proves ineffectual, we repair to the school board. Yelling and screaming all the way in defense of kids not our own, we parents can have great impact on making our campuses safer than they are. When we defend our own, we react to "an instance." When we defend the other kid, we react to "the issue." And a matter of "an issue" is far more forceful than a matter of "an instance."

Discern if your child is being bullied at home. Sometimes a father bullies his children, mistakenly believing he is "just teasing" them or "toughening them up." Don't do it. Children who are bullied at home will either become victims of bullies outside the home or learn to be bullies themselves.

If Your Child Is a Bully

All boys grow through a stage (junior high through high school) where they need to see themselves as skillful, if not outright swashbuckling, mini-gladiators and warriors. Part of normal male development is to play the primitive game of "King o' the Hill" where the object is to capture through physical force the summit of a mound and keep others from wresting it from him. The school ground is a boy's little summit, his fiefdom, and some children will throw their weight around to keep control, usually overcoming those who are smaller, younger, and less aggressive. Many adults see bullying as a normal part of growing up. It is not. Parents and teachers are usually not aware of the problem, or they ignore it. After all, "boys will be boys."

Around the sophomore or junior year of high school the competitive animal should give way to the cooperative, flexible, self-adjusting social being. Before that, though, the male needs to feel masterful, forceful, and powerful, but not to the extent that others must suffer.

Most males grow through this stage, but others feel compelled to make their whole world an enlarged field for the playing of the game. They never outgrow it. By the time they are in high school, and even into college or the workplace, their form of bullying becomes physically and mentally terrifying to their victims. Several conditions seem to turn children into bullies.

School-age bullies experience abuse at home. A child who is a bully at school is usually abused in some way or neglected at home. He often experiences rejection beginning in early childhood and may be subject to extensive physical punishment. He is abused by his parents or older siblings or frequently witnesses spousal abuse.

He soon learns that aggression and violence are methods of getting his own way.

Bullies are generally larger in size than their peers and tend to consistently exhibit aggressive behavior. Such behavior is learned; in fact, patterns for aggressive conduct are often set by the time a child is eight years old, according to research by Dr. Leonard Eron, a professor at the University of Illinois, Chicago.[13]

Since "experts" lean toward looking at the home environment for children's becoming bullies, parents may be reluctant to recognize—or else they are not aware—that their children are bullies.

They receive inconsistent punishment, or extreme and harsh discipline. Inconsistency in discipline methods causes a child to be confused about his parents' expectations of him. One time he gets pounded for one small act of orneriness or disobedience, another time he is ignored when he does something really bad. Parents should agree on discipline standards and stick to them. Most of the time, children will respond to correction without harsh physical punishment.

Some are generally ignored by their parents. Some parents of bullies tend to ignore their children. These parents are so caught up in their own lives that they pay little attention to what their children do, where they go, who their friends are, or what their emotional needs may be. Their children have too little love and care at home and too much freedom.

Bullies learn violence by watching violent television programs. Studies indicate that young children learn to dominate others by watching movies and TV programs that depict aggressive behavior. Contrary to popular opinion, watching violence or aggression is not an acceptable outlet for pent-up hostilities. Rather it teaches children how better to perform aggressive acts, reduces their inhibitions against aggression, desensitizes the bully to violence, and proves to them that bullying is a successful form of social interaction.

They lack negotiating skills. Dr. Ronald Slaby, a Harvard psychologist who has studied bullies, suggests that there are many non-aggressive ways to defend yourself: negotiating; ignoring; talking back without provoking—in general, just standing up for your rights and holding your ground.[14] Perhaps you could suggest that your school provide a workshop for children who tend to be victims or who feel they must bully in order to defend their turf. For further help, contact the National School Safety Center, c/o Pepperdine University, Malibu, CA 90263 (805) 373-9977.

They don't know how to act without aggression. Dr. Nathanial Floyd, a psychologist for the Board of Cooperative Educational Services of Southern Westchester, New York, says that some people seem to "need a victim and may work hard to create a victim, even if there isn't one."[15] When these aggressive children perceive vulnerability in another child they feel threatened because they are reminded of painful times when they were humiliated, shamed, or victimized.

It is important to stop your child from being a bully as early as you can. Young bullies are more likely to become maladjusted as adults and to suffer from family and professional problems.

Schools Must Assume Some of the Responsibility

All fifty states have laws that require teachers to report incidents of child abuse to the appropriate child protective services agency in their community. Bullying is a form of child abuse and should be handled as such. Furthermore, school officials should take positive steps to appropriately supervise children in their care and provide training programs that teach conflict-resolution skills.

Fifty percent of school-yard bullies grow up to become criminals; 25 percent are serious criminals.[16] We can identify these youngsters as early as kindergarten and first grade, but we tend to do little about them.

Whether your child is a victim or a bully, or if you are aware of such children in your circle of friends or your neighborhood, perhaps you could intervene to see that these children get help through the school system. If it is not done early in the child's life, it will be too late by the time he reaches adolescence.

Bullying can be stopped through careful and sensitive intervention. In 1987, a dozen internationally renowned researchers from the fields of psychology, education, law enforcement, and public relations gathered at the first-ever "Schoolyard Bully Practicum" at Harvard University to formulate a plan for combating this pervasive problem. The National School Safety Center, a partnership of the U.S. Departments of Justice and Education and Pepperdine University, sponsored the practicum. For information, write the National School Safety Center, c/o Pepperdine University, Malibu, CA 90263 (805) 373-9977.

You may need to get personally and physically involved. At one inner-city high school that has been plagued with student violence, the principal has developed parent participation strategies to deal with campus aggression. The goal is to have at least twelve volunteer parents per day helping supervise playgrounds, hallways, restrooms, and other potential problem areas. Merely having a parent present in the back of a classroom, "just smiling," has done wonders for the teaching quality, too. And the program has not cost the district a dime.[17]

Even those children or youths who are not themselves targets of aggression but who witness it, or who are simply afraid of what could happen to them, are still affected by the environment of terror that menaces the whole school and disturbs the peace necessary for an adequate education.

Get rid of the fallacy that kids who fight each other are just experiencing normal youthful aggressive behavior. Kids abusing other kids or creating their own tyranny based on their strength, their group, or their power over the weak cannot be considered a normal part of the process of growing up.

One thing that parents may not be aware of is their child's legal right to safety at school. In an article entitled "Victims Can Sue Bullies, Schools," Donna Clontz, former general counsel for the National School Safety Center, says that "an unprovoked beating is a criminal act called battery." If your child comes home beaten up, you have legal recourse to sue the school—if the school authorities are aware that a student is a bully and has done nothing to protect other children from him or her; they can also sue the bully's parents.[18]

We tend to get not only what we expect, what we deserve, and what we ask for, but perhaps most significantly, we get what we "put up with." To stop bullying, parents and teachers must communicate to children that bullying will not be tolerated. At the same time, we need to teach children and youths the kinds of skills they need to get along well with others. Parents and community leaders should work with school officials to develop effective *intervention* strategies to bring the problem under control, and *prevention* strategies to work with those bent on a pattern of bullying behavior.

What Works

Kids should know that *everyone* gets picked on in some way, at some time. Teach them how to handle it when they are young.

1. Assume we're probably getting picked on. Don't wait for us to tell you about it.

2. Take us seriously. Take action on our behalf.

3. Teach us to walk tall: "I'm not afraid of you!" The kids who get picked on continually are the ones who show fear. It's no fun to pick on someone who doesn't cry or get scared or run away.

What Doesn't Work

1. If parents or teachers bully kids, we do not toughen up, we become more victimized.

2. Teachers who ridicule or make fun of a student who is already being bullied reinforce our feelings of helplessness.

6

Gangs

Human beings love to join groups, be part of exclusive clubs, be affiliated with others who like the same things they like, to feel accepted, to belong. We start very young, dividing up into cliques and clubs, and gradually progress into fraternities, sororities, interest groups, unions, federations, societies, lodges, leagues, and chapters. Somewhere along the way—and it is happening at earlier ages than ever before—some of us join gangs.

When Billy turned twelve he knew he would have to become one of the "Bangers." He did not have a choice. He knew he would get beaten up by the Bangers until he joined or he would get beaten up by the "Poppers," the rival gang, whenever they got him alone without protection. "All the kids join the Bangers when they get into PS 112," Billy explained. "No one says no to Jimmy [the Banger's gang leader, who did time once for nearly killing another Banger with an Uzi]. You don't mess with Jimmy. He'd just as soon kill you as look at you."

Besides, Billy says, "When I put on my Banger jacket, I feel really *bad.*" Billy's eyes sparkle.[1]

The Bangers are nothing like the old "Our Gang" depicted in early movies; neither are they like Huckleberry Finn and Tom Sawyer swearing a blood-alliance. And gangs have no similarity to one of the oldest organizations for boys, the Boy Scouts. The goal of the Bangers is not good deeds, and only wimps meet in a tree-house club. But being a member of the Bangers helps you to feel proud and safe. It is like having older brothers who will protect you. To be a Banger is to be big and threatening, someone who matters and has to be reckoned with. Bangers have power and status. They have secret hand signs and other signals nobody else knows about.

What's wrong with that? Kids need to feel accepted, to have rites and rituals, to receive the approval of their peers. Being part of a gang is not new. But today's gangs are something else, they have gone amok. The only way to stem this treacherous trend that is spreading across America is for parents, educators, law enforcers, legislators, judges, prosecutors, community leaders, the media, and the general public to join together to fight it.

Are There Gangs in Your Community?

Concerned parents get involved with their children's schools. They ask if there is gang activity around their community. The following "Gang Assessment Tool" determines how severe a gang problem is in your community.

1.   *Do you have graffiti on or near your campus?* (5 points) Graffiti is one of the first warning signs of gang activity. It is more than a form of vandalism; it is a way to communicate, intimidate, and delineate turf control.

2.   *Do you have crossed-out graffiti on or near your campus?* (10 points) Crossed-out graffiti means that there is more than one gang in the community and that the likelihood for gang warfare is more prominent.

3.   *Do your students wear colors, jewelry, clothing, or flash hand signals or display other behavior that may be gang related?* (10 points) More and more school districts are establishing dress codes that prohibit the wearing of gang

symbols, gang colors, do-rags, or disruptive dress styles.
Parents should particularly be aware of these gang styles
and make certain their children do not wear them. It is
too easy to be mistaken for a gang member and end up
as another statistic.

4. *Are drugs available near your school?* (5 points) One
    student was asked, "Do you have a drug problem in your
    school?" She replied, "No, I can get all the drugs I want."
    Drugs and gangs are inseparably related. Gangs have
    experts in drug dealing, marketing, money laundering,
    and franchising. Many gangs today are about more than
    affiliation. They are about money. A group of Los Ange-
    les gang members, recently caught by law enforcement
    officials in St. Louis, was conducting a drug sales semi-
    nar.[2] Gangs are on the move and looking for opportuni-
    ties to come into communities where they can get more
    money for their drugs, where it is easier to intimidate,
    where law enforcement is less prepared, and where there
    is less gang rivalry.

5. *Has there been a significant increase in the number of
    physical confrontations or stare-downs within the past
    twelve months in or near your school?* (5 points) Fights
    symbolize the increasing conflict that exists on many
    campuses. School violence and intimidation encourage
    the formation of gangs and gang-related activity.

6. *Is there an increasing presence of weapons in your
    school or community?* (10 points) Weapons are tools of
    the trade. Wherever you find gangs, you will usually find
    weapons. Unfortunately, when a weapon is used, it cre-
    ates an irreversible consequence. A fistfight is one thing,
    but a gunfight can result in tragedy.

7. *Are beepers, pagers, or cellular phones used by your students?* (10 points) Most schools outlaw the use of such devices for students. Except in rare cases, beepers and pagers do not belong on students in school.

8. *Has there been a drive-by shooting at or near your school?* (15 points) Drive-by shootings and walk-by beatings are becoming more common. If there have been drive-by shootings near the school grounds, it means that conditions are grave and gang activity in your community has graduated to its most serious state.

9. *Have you had a "show-by" display of weapons at or around your school?* (10 points) Usually, before a drive-by shooting occurs, there will be a "show-by"—a flashing of weapons.

10. *Is your truancy rate increasing?* (15 points) There is a high correlation between truancy and daytime burglary, as high as 70 percent in some communities. Youngsters who are not in school are often terrorizing the community. When you go to work, they go to work. When you get home, you find out how well they did.

11. *Are racial incidents increasing in your community or school?* (5 points) There is a direct correlation between gang membership and racial conflict. Many gangs form along racial and ethnic lines for protection, affiliation, respect, and appreciation. Sometimes, however, these affiliations breed criminal acts of violence and intimidation. It is important for us to teach our children to understand and respect ethnic and racial differences rather than to fear and feel threatened by them.

12. *Is there a history of gang activity in your community?* (10 points) Gangs are not a new phenomenon. They have

been around for decades—in some cases, several generations. If your community has a history of gangs, your
children are much more likely to be influenced by them.

13. *Is there an increase in "informal social groups" in your
school or community with unusual names like the Wood-
land Heights Posse; Rip Off and Rule; Kappa Phi Nasty;
18th Street Crew; or Females Simply Chillin?* (15 points)
The development of hard-core gang members often begins
with innocent yet revealing name identifications. These
innocent clubs can become primary recruiting targets for
hard-core gang members.

A score of fifty points or more indicates a need to develop a
gang prevention and intervention plan. If you score above 70 points
you have a severe gang problem. Zero-20 is insignificant; 25–45
reflects an emerging gang problem.[3]

Whether gang activity is just beginning in your community or
is already out of control, you as a parent can do something about
curbing its increase. Supervision is critical. Chicago residents have
parent patrols that escort youngsters to and from school. Orange
County, California, parents have a similar program called "Opera-
tion Safe Corridors." Many junior and senior high schools have
parent volunteers visit the school and provide extra supervision on
playgrounds, in hallways, restrooms, and other potential trouble
areas.

Get educated about gang mentality. One mother, for instance,
could not understand why her son, who had a size 32 waist, wanted
her to buy him size 44 pants. Baggy pants were simply a sign of
gang affiliation. You can conceal a lot of contraband, including
weapons, in baggy clothing. (However, wanting to wear baggy
clothes doesn't always indicate gang activity.)

Question where your child goes. An answer of "out" is not
good enough. Find out where he is going, whom he will be with,
when he will be home. Gangs sponsor certain functions for their

members. Know where your children spend their time. Ask questions. Investigate the activity. Get involved in your child's free time.

As soon as you detect evidence of any gang activity in your child's school or community, you need to begin to teach your child the difference between belonging to an acceptable group of kids with similar interests and joining a gang. It may take a hearty investment of your time at first to work through this issue with your children, but the payoff is invaluable.

Why Do Kids Join Gangs?

Why is there such an increase in gang membership? Young children and teens are often attracted to gangs because they:

- have low self-esteem.
- come from dysfunctional families (hopelessness, substance abuse, child abuse, divorce, workaholism, and/or lack of nurturing).
- have little or no adult supervision and guidance.
- suffer from economic and social stress.
- lack personal and social responsibility.
- feel frustrated.
- are victims.
- feel alienated.
- cannot see any alternatives.
- are surrounded by negative peer pressure.
- are weak or failing academically.
- have not learned adequate coping skills.[4]

Your children need to see gang membership for what it is, a dangerous, deadly lifestyle that can lead to serious injury, prison, or death. They may affiliate with a gang, believing they can quit anytime they want to, but quitting is not always an option. Gang membership usually means blood-in/blood-out.

Educators Lopez and Garrison outline how parents can help their children resist gang influence. While these suggestions were made to educators, they can also be implemented by parents even before children reach school age.

Your child's behavior reflects his feelings and attitudes. Emotions are powerful enforcers that demand action. If your child feels that she is important, that she is worthwhile, she will avoid doing anything that may bring harm to herself or to others. Children should understand that:

- Feelings are. We do not have a choice in whether or not to have feelings. All healthy humans have emotions and feelings.

- Feelings are neither good nor bad, but simply part of us.

- We are responsible for what we do with our feelings, but not for having feelings.

- We can identify our feelings and deal with them consciously and constructively.

Your son or daughter needs to practice getting in touch with feelings. Ask your child what makes him happy, what makes him sad, what makes him angry or upsets him. Tell him to close his eyes and imagine that he is happy and describe how he feels. Then ask him to imagine that he is angry. What does his anger make him feel like doing to himself or to others? By understanding how emotions such as fear, anger, hostility, stress, or guilt can cause us to react in destructive ways, we can learn to control our behavior during emotional times. When we let these emotions control us, they become dangerous to our well-being.

Your child should build good, strong self-esteem. Self-esteem is the value we place on our own personal worth, how we evaluate ourselves. Our self-esteem level is reflected in our behavior. In other words, when your child does something positive and receives praise and appreciation for this positive action, his self- esteem level raises a notch or two. He feels good about himself and wants to continue the positive action.

A young child needs continuous positive reinforcement of her self-worth if she is to gain a level of self-esteem that will carry her through the turmoils of growing up. A child who likes and believes in herself and sees that she is a good, worthwhile person will generally not feel the need to belong to a negative support group, such as a gang.

To teach her to think well of herself, ask her what she likes about herself. Have her tell you what she does well. Also find out what she does not like about herself. Teach her that all of us have characteristics or physical "flaws" that we don't like in ourselves, but if we think only about our imperfections we soon forget the many good qualities we have. Eventually, these good qualities will be overshadowed by our bad qualities and we will begin to live out only the bad things we see in ourselves.

Your child needs to learn how to relax. Children are often filled with unexpressed fears. They are victimized, stressed, confused, and frustrated, just as their parents are. Children in this generation are exposed to violence of every kind in movies and on TV, and they are not always able to separate the make-believe from the real.

Some of your young child's worst fears will never invade his life, but he still fears getting seriously hurt, being kidnapped, shot, or abandoned. He worries that one of his parents will die or they will separate and divorce. He fears that, like Cinderella, Snow White, and Hansel and Gretel, he will get a stepparent or stepbrothers and stepsisters. He worries about commonplace things that happen to almost everyone. He fears the first day of school, losing his lunch, forgetting where his next class is or his locker combination, losing (or forgetting to do) his homework. He worries about being lost in a crowd, getting separated from you. He is afraid of the dog that barks at him when he walks home from school and the big, boisterous kid who picks on the little guys.

You can help your child learn to relax and not be so anxious about things that may never happen, or learn to handle these threatening situations.

- Listen to your child's fears. Treat them as if they are real concerns. Assure him that some of the things he fears will never happen to him, and that even if some of his fears do become fact, he can learn to cope.

- Take time regularly to help your child imagine a quiet place where he has been or a peaceful scene in a picture. Tell him to close his eyes and imagine he is sitting in this quiet place where he smells clean air, hears happy sounds, feels warm and safe. Show him that he can escape to this quiet place whenever he feels afraid or anxious. He will soon learn that when his mind is at rest he can see his fears for what they are. He will discover that he can overcome irrational fears or solve real problems.

- Help him explore ways to solve problems without using violence. Suggest alternatives to lashing out or running away when he feels afraid, such as the following.

Children need to learn how to set goals and achieve them. A wise parent will begin early in a child's life to give her responsibilities and choices so she can learn to be self-reliant. Part of this training is to teach how to set goals. Children need to see themselves as achievers and winners. Many Olympic athletes use this technique in their training: They picture themselves standing in the winner's box, receiving their commendation. This helps them to compete more effectively and securely.

Even young children can be taught to set goals by using the SMART formula: A goal should be Specific, Measurable, Attainable, Realistic, and have a Time limit. Playing with building blocks and Tinkertoys involves goal setting. Stacking blocks twenty high is a specific, measurable, attainable goal that is realistic and can be done within a time limit. A school-age child can set a goal to get an A in spelling. Achieving these goals is what builds self-confidence so that your child can increase and enlarge the scope of his goals. Encourage your child when he fails to reach a goal within his time limit, and praise him when he accomplishes his goal.

Children need to know and be able to use good communication skills. Communication begins at birth. David Augsburger describes early communication between a mother and infant:

> Morning breaks. At the first sounds from the nursery the mother enters and begins the daily greeting ritual. Cooing, talking, testing for wetness or dryness, holding, stroking, reassuring, and calling the child by name. This is the beginning of what will be a constant human need for the rest of life. We humans have a central need for consistent recognition and certification: I am known and am named. I am one with those I love. I am separate and recognized as such. I am part of my family. I am separate and distinct as a person.[5]

A child who is respected and communicated with at home will generally not seek outside arenas, such as gangs, where he can have a say.

Everyone has opinions and ideas, even very young children. These points of view are important and should be shared with others. To do this effectively requires that we know how to communicate—verbally and non-verbally. Listening and respecting the views of others completes the communication process. Listening with an open mind to what other people feel and believe and sharing what we believe can go a long way toward resolving conflicts within ourselves and with others.

Children need to develop positive relationships and utilize positive support groups. As we said at the beginning of this chapter, everyone needs to feel included, to be part of a whole. Encourage your child to get involved in an organized sport, special group, or service club at school, church, or in the community. What are his interests? Maybe your son or daughter could join a drama club, league of some kind, the Boy Scouts, Campfire Girls, Little

League, a service club, swimming team, computer club.... Research the organizations in your community.

Joining with kids who have similar interests creates a feeling of strength, of achievement, of belonging. Kids who are active in positive organizations do not feel the pressure or desire to become part of a negative organization, such as a gang. Inner-city leaders have discovered that children and youths involved in athletics or youth centers do not feel the need to join gangs.

If your community does not have organizations such as these, band together with other concerned parents and begin some. If one organization does not appeal to your child, find another one where he or she feels at home with kids of similar interests.

Children need to learn good leadership skills. Possessing good leadership skills does not necessarily mean you learn to lead and control others, but it means you can lead and direct your own life and control your own thinking. Leadership skills help you develop personal power.

Perhaps you have noticed that a person who appears to "have it all together" seems confident within himself and knows where he is going and is often surrounded by other people. People naturally gravitate to him. He has a following even if he did not start out to be a leader. Such a person seldom seems influenced by peer pressure. No one ever approaches him about getting involved in anything that is not good and positive because he acts determined, committed, and secure in his own decision-making process. This person has good leadership skills. How do you instill these skills in your child?

- Encourage her to think for herself. A child who is constantly told to do what you say simply "because I told you to" will not learn self–discipline and leadership skills. It is only one small step to doing what an older gang leader tells her to do. Explain why certain demands are made of her. She will soon learn to question, to challenge, to argue, to think for herself.

- Compliment and reinforce your child when she is creative and accomplishes something new and different.

- Show your child that she is responsible for what she thinks and how she behaves. She cannot blame anyone else for her thought patterns or her actions. When she realizes that the consequences of her behavior fall on her own shoulders, she will begin to take leadership over her thought processes and her life.

Children need to learn socially responsible rites and rituals to replace those that perpetuate gang membership. Kids love special rites and rituals. Gangs have them, as well as special symbols, hand signals, colors, and initiations—things that movies glamorize and kids idealize.[6]

Another thing that appeals to young people is the initiation ceremony. All gangs have some kind of initiation for new recruits. "Gang initiations often require a new member to prove his worth and fearlessness. The most common induction test requires the initiate to fight several established members. Sometimes the potential members must commit a purse snatching or robbery or a more violent crime."[7]

To these eight needs we would add one more:

Parents should limit their children's exposure to violence. This is difficult if you live in a neighborhood where violence is an everyday fact. But those who live in small cities, towns, and suburbs see violence as well: in movies and on television. In a series of articles entitled "Growing Up in America," Ron Harris, staff writer for the *Los Angeles Times*, reported:

> In 1969, the first full year of the movie-rating system, 81 movies were rated G, for general audiences, 139 were rated M, for mature audiences, and 83 were rated R, for restricted. [In 1990], there were only eight G-rated movies. Another 168 were rated PG—the replacement for M—and 341 were rated R.[8]

Newsweek reported: "By the age of 18, the average American child will have seen 200,000 violent acts on television, including 40,000 murders. . . . The average two- to eleven-year-old watches TV twenty-five hours a week."[9] The author went on to report that Leonard Eron and L. Rowell Huesmann, psychologists at the University of Illinois, studied a set of children for twenty years. Those kids who watched "significant amounts of television" when they were eight years old were more likely to commit violent crimes when they were thirty — including child and spousal abuse. These experts believe

> heavy exposure to televised violence is one of the causes of aggressive behavior, crime, and violence in society. . . . Television violence affects youngsters of all ages, of both genders, at all socioeconomic levels, and all levels of intelligence. . . . It cannot be denied or explained away.[10]

Motion pictures and television are not the only places where children and young people are exposed to violence. Modern rock music promotes uncontrolled sex, alcohol, drugs, defiance of authority, preoccupation with death, and the occult, including Satanism. Parents need to be aware of the messages, beliefs, and values portrayed by much of today's youth music. Kids love music and dance. Expose them to music that will instill high moral values. Much music is available today with the beat they want to dance to and the lyrics you want them to listen to.

School Involvement with Youth Gangs

School officials are becoming more aware of their need to develop gang prevention strategies for several reasons. Schools are prime recruiting grounds; schools are open markets for drug selling; gang members stake out specific school areas as their turf and control access to or use of those areas. This gives the gangs a sense of power and ownership. Whenever their turf is trespassed upon, it usually results in violence on campus. Gang members extort fees from students who want to use certain school facilities that are in their turf, or who need to walk through their claimed areas to get to school. They even charge for "protection" so the student does not get hurt.

Desperate parents and educators continue to come up with suggestions on how to discourage gang activity in schools. Dr. Lilia Lopez implemented an anti-gang curriculum in California in September of 1990. Called Mission SOAR (Set Objectives Achieve Results), it focuses on building positive self- esteem, achieving goals, and practicing group problem-solving.

The Los Angeles County Sheriff has also developed an anti-gang curriculum modeled after the Substance Abuse and Narcotic Education (SANE) program. DARE (Drug Abuse Resistance Education) has recently added two lessons on gang prevention. Similar programs are being developed in other public school systems.

School officials also recognize that victims who report gang activity need to be supported and protected. If students and staff members do not feel safe in reporting gang crimes, the situation will only worsen. Some schools provide in-service training and gang counseling services as a way to support victims and potential victims of gang violence and intimidation.

Strengthen Your Family Unit

Following are ideas that will help you raise your family so that each child will develop the inner strength he or she needs to avoid becoming involved with a gang.

Make house rules and other rules to live by.

- Establish behavior expectations and explain reasons for each rule.

- Rules should involve your children's safety. Explain how they do.

- You yourself as the parent must also live by and reinforce the rules and principles you teach.

- Set a good example. Children are followers. They will mimic your example even if you tell them they must behave differently.

- Punish from a cool head and a warm heart.

Don't relinquish your role as parent.

- It is okay to be your child's friend, but you are his parent first and foremost. Sometimes you need to pull rank and lay down or back up the house rules.

- Children have to obey. You need to see to it that they do.

- When your children reach the age of twelve or thirteen, shift your parenting style from boss to wise enabler, one who comes into a child's life softly and by invitation, who without coercive method, suggests alternatives with explanations, who then makes an offer to help the child implement them. The wise enabler makes happen things that a child could only dream about by creating special memories.

- Parenting is never convenient or easy. Make sure your rules are for the good of your child, not just what makes life easier for you.

- Stay on duty. Never fall asleep for a moment. Your job as a parent is to be a lifeguard in shark-infested waters.

- Remember that your parenting responsibility is at least a twenty-year project. If you do it right to begin with, the enjoyable part starts thirteen or fourteen years after the beginning. Do not expect parenting to be a picnic all the time. Actually, the parenting success we enjoy with our children is like the investment theory of work—our output is directly related to our input.

- Parenting is exhausting work with little payback for a long time. To expect anything else will frustrate you and your children, causing screeching collisions of wills, needs, and expectations.

Be an integral part of your children's lives.

- Keep communication lines open.

- Get involved in your children's world.

- Get to know their friends.

- Get to know their friends' parents.

- Spend time with your kids.

- Every once in a while, renew acquaintance with your kids. Children change over time and you need to keep up with the changes.

Be human.

- Admit mistakes when you make them. Children need to hear that you are sometimes wrong.

- Learn to laugh at yourself and at your children.

- Be warm, loving, considerate, approachable, courteous, respectful of your children. Example teaches better than lecture.

Show them that you care for them and about what happens to them.

- Hug your children—a lot.

- If your children have to be latchkey kids, phone them frequently so that they can sense your closeness and concern.

- Find out what they are interested in and become a supplier or provider of those interests. Do not decide for them what they should be interested in and shove them toward your goals. They will resist you just as you would resist someone forcing you into a path you do not want to follow.

- Teach discipline and responsibility by being disciplined and responsible yourself first and then seeing to it that they stick to their chosen activity long enough to accomplish something.

- Be their biggest fan and let them know you are. Tell them you are proud of them when they accomplish what they set out to do.

- Praise them. Send praise notes and cards to them often.

- Be willing to defer your own activity for awhile to listen to your child when he has something exciting and neat to tell you about his world.

- Remember that your children are not here to cater to your expectations or demands. They have their own agendas, which you must respect.

- Go out of your way to do nice things for your children.

- Do not deplete all your niceness and patience during your busy day. Save some for your children when you hit the front door and encounter a barrage of parenting chores and kid requests.

- Beware of the philosophy that says you must look after yourself first so that you will be good for your kids. You will have to look out for their best interests first for a long time. This is not to say that you are to indulge them, or completely disregard your own needs, but that their needs should come before yours. Arrange, or rearrange, your priorities to reflect their needs.

- Provide a moral, religious, spiritual network around them so that they recognize the existence of a Supreme Being—God—who is always available to hear them, help them, comfort them, and sustain them when they may feel that their parents have failed them.

Encourage your child's innate belief in God. Robert Coles, a psychiatrist and professor at Harvard University, has spent his life studying children. He is the author of eight books, including *The Spiritual Life of Children*. Dr. Coles said that he was surprised to find that children, whether from religious or atheistic families, think about faith. They try to figure out what is happening to them and why. Amidst it all is a firm belief in God. He wrote, "During my years in child psychiatry and pediatrics, I grossly underestimated how significant religion is in the lives of children."[11]

Children accept the fact of a God who cares for them and will keep this faith until it is beaten, ridiculed, or argued out of them.

What Works

The reason most people join gangs is to be part of a family and for protection. If we already have families, we won't feel this need so much. Maybe a small school would be better for us. Becoming involved in small-group activities, such as school clubs, helps us feel this "family" feeling, too.

7

Drugs

O ne evening, in a small central California coastal valley, two high school girlfriends were at one of the girl's homes getting ready to attend a school dance. The mother noticed that her daughter's friend seemed overly giggly, and she suspected that the girl was on alcohol or drugs. After the girls left for the dance, she called the other mother and expressed her concern. The two women went to the dance and privately challenged their daughters with their suspicion. Even though the girls denied any involvement, the mothers felt their suspicions were justified and committed themselves to do what they could to protect their children. Beer drinking had long been a problem in the valley, resulting in many deaths and serious injuries among teenagers, but not much had been revealed concerning drug use or dealing.

The two mothers contacted several other parents, and the group met to discuss what many of them had suspected was a growing problem: alcohol and drug use among teenagers. The parents contacted school authorities who, at first, were reluctant to admit there could be a problem. Finally, through persistence and commitment, a parent support network was formed to investigate and eliminate this potential disaster to their children. The network focused on three primary actions:

One, to meet together once a month and learn about drugs,

how they affect a person, and how to detect if their children were using them. Former drug users told of their experiences and the sheriff's department showed drug paraphernalia.

Two, to take turns standing guard around the school grounds. Students were not allowed to leave campus during school breaks without a pass, and no non-student was allowed on campus without a valid reason for being there.

Three, to get to know the parents of their children's friends. They began checking with one another to make sure their children were properly chaperoned at parties and generally supervised at all times.

After a couple of years of spirited "watch-dogging," several students, parents, and school authorities attended the National Federation of Parents for Drug-Free Youth in Washington, D.C., to share with organizations from other parts of the nation what they were doing about the drug problem in their valley. This initial parent support group became recognized as the nation's seventh most effective anti-drug program, called Network for Drug-Free Youth; those six programs ahead of this small community effort were based in larger cities with more financial support.

As we work with school-aged children around the country we often ask the question, "Is there a drug problem in your school?" A common response is, "No, I can get all the drugs I want!"

More than ever before, children are getting caught in the web of drug experimentation and use, and they are doing so at far younger ages. Drug pushers and dealers are taking advantage of the fact that children in this generation have easy access to spending money. Those youths and children in the inner cities, whose parents cannot afford to give allowances and spending money, are encouraged by drug pushers to sell drugs so they can make more money than they ever could by working at honest jobs.

What Drugs Do Children Have Access To?

A *drug* is any chemical substance that brings about physical, emotional, or mental changes in a person. This includes alcohol, nicotine, caffeine, tetrahydrocannibinol (THC, in marijuana and hashish), amphetamines, barbiturates, tranquilizers, narcotics, cocaine, phencyclidin (PCP), volatile chemicals (glue and other inhalants), and lysergic acid diethylamide (LSD).

Drug abuse is the use of any chemical substance, legal or illegal, that causes physical, mental, emotional, or social harm to the user or to those close to the user.

The best way to control drug abuse is by prevention—meaning that you educate your family so that no member is ever drawn into drug use.

Drugs fall into several classifications: stimulants, depressants, narcotics, intoxicants, and hallucinogens. Some of these drugs are legal; most are illegal. Many of them are in your home, such as coffee, tea, and chocolate, and most refrigerators contain beer or wine in some form or other. We all know the positive effect a cup of coffee has on us when we get out of bed in the morning. Caffeine is a drug, a "stimulant." It will not cause physical, mental, emotional, or social harm to anyone who hangs around a coffee drinker. However, many people have been warned by their doctors that caffeine is not good for them physically.

The stimulant nicotine in tobacco, on the other hand, according to reports by the surgeon general of the United States, not only harms the user but also threatens persons around the one doing the smoking. Other drugs classified as stimulants may also be found in your own home; capsules or pills containing Benzedrine, Desoxyn, Dexedrine, and Byphetamine are used to treat various medical problems (even weight reduction). These drugs go by the slang names of Uppers, Pep Pills, Wake-ups, Bennies, Peaches, Hearts, Meth, Speed, or Oranges.

Alcohol, a "depressant-intoxicant," is physically harmful to the user, and in the case of a drunken driver or one who tends to be violent when drunk, an alcohol abuser certainly endangers the lives of others. Other depressants include barbiturates such as Nembutal and Seconal (Downers, Goof Balls, Barbs, Candy, Peanuts, Yellows, Reds). These are sedatives and are found in prescription drugs. There are also non-barbiturate depressants such as Noctec, Equanil,

Miltown, Noludar, Doriden, Placidyl, Quaalude, Valium, and Librium, which are tranquilizers, muscle relaxants, and sleeping pills. These are popular drugs found in homes of people who suffer sleeplessness, anxiety, tension, high blood pressure, or illnesses in which seizures and convulsions occur, and are also used as muscle relaxers.

Those drugs that fall in the loosely used "narcotic" classification include cocaine (Snow, Dust, Flake, Girl, Bernice, Cecil, C, Coke); heroin (Horse, H, Smack, Boy, Junk, Hard Stuff, Sugar, Lipton Tea, Joy Powder, Dope); methadone (Dollies, Dolls); morphine (Morpho, M, Emsil, Unkie, Hocus, Miss Emma, White Stuff, Junk, Dope). Medically, these drugs are used as anesthetics and pain relievers, and methadone is used in withdrawal therapy from other narcotics.

Cocaine use has tripled among young adults during the last few years.[1]

Marijuana, the most widely used illegal drug, is classified as an intoxicant. While there are some definite medical benefits to marijuana, the dangerous side-effects far outweigh the benefits. Of the four hundred known chemicals found in marijuana, sixty-one of these are cannabinoids which affect the central nervous system. This effect on the nervous system shows up in the user's lack of ability to express complex ideas, difficulty in concentration, irregular sleeping habits, unexpected mood changes, minimized psychomotor performance, and irregular visual perception.[2]

Marijuana also has adverse effects on the brain. Researchers have proven that marijuana interferes with immediate memory and intellectual performance. It can impair concentration and reading comprehension. It affects the heart and lungs, just as tobacco does, and has a higher concentration of known cancer-causing agents than tobacco has.

Marijuana affects the body's reproductive system. Males who use it daily have a lower sperm count than those who do not. It can reduce the body's production of the male hormone, testosterone. THC, the chief intoxicant in marijuana, has caused birth defects in laboratory animals and may cause birth defects in humans. Mothers who smoke marijuana and nurse their babies risk harming their children with THC. If that is not enough, studies on both humans and laboratory animals show that marijuana also affects the body's immune system.

Intoxicant users exhibit euphoria, mood swings, increased appetite, confusion, and drunkenness. Those who sniff organic intoxicants may be nauseated, vomit, hallucinate, or have transient psychoses.   Intoxicants include aerosols, airplane glue, gasoline, paint thinners, lighter fluid, and other inhalants that cause mental confusion. Regular use of these intoxicants—whether deliberately or through constant exposure in work areas—causes permanent organic damage to the lungs, brain, liver, and bone marrow.

The final drug classification is "hallucinogens." This includes lysergic acid diethylamide (LSD, Acid); phencyclidine (PCP, Angel Dust); and Mescaline. Users experience hallucinations, panic, depression, confusion, and irrational behavior. An overdose can cause convulsions, coma, and death. Use of LSD may cause birth defects.

Even years after a person has quit using the drug he can suffer "flashbacks" of the effects. PCP was originally developed as a powerful animal tranquilizer and an anesthetic for surgery. Doctors abandoned its use with humans when it was discovered that it caused bizarre effects in the person being treated.

All of these drugs are available in the United States, legally or illegally. All of them are highly dangerous.

How Can You Know If Your Child Is Using Drugs?

In addition to the symptoms listed above, you should be aware of the following: A person on stimulants will be excitable, restless, confused, or depressed. He may have tremors, insomnia, or hallucinations. Continued use can destroy nasal membranes, cause heart problems, malnutrition, lesions in the lungs, and even death.

A person who abuses drugs is in danger of overdosing because a user is not in full control of his actions.

Continued use can lead to a real psychological and/or physical need for the drugs. Long-term use can destroy a healthy body and mind. It can lead to damaged organs, mental illness, and malnutrition. When anyone is under the influence of any drug that takes away his self-control, he can become over-confident and take foolish risks that jeopardize not only his own life but also the lives of those around him. Added to these physical problems are the legal, economic, and personal ones.

If you discover that your child is abusing any kind of drug, you should immediately get outside help. In many cases, breaking a drug habit without professional help can be dangerous because of withdrawal symptoms, and difficult because of the psychological need. Outside professional help may include medical supervision, rehabilitation, methadone maintenance, use of new blocking drugs, counseling, and therapeutic communities.

There are many agencies, both public and private, that you can turn to if your child is abusing drugs. These include drug treatment centers and clinics, hospitals, mental health centers, public health agencies, halfway houses, detoxification centers, and Alcoholics Anonymous. Look in the Yellow Pages of your phone book under "Drug Abuse," "Addiction," or "Alcoholism" for specific organizations in your areas.

Why Do Kids Use Drugs?

Peer Pressure. The single most important source of social influence is the peer system. One of the most basic of human psychological needs is to belong to a group. People will twist themselves into all kinds of shapes to fit into a group for the sake of belonging. "Fitting in" somewhere in the social order of things is a powerful driving force in every child's life.

So that I (McDill) can demonstrate how powerful peer pressure or influence is, at some time during a lecture I ask the group to imagine the emotional effect of standing up in a church service while the pastor is delivering a sermon and, in a clear and bold voice, beginning to recite the Pledge of Allegiance. In some twenty years of asking for volunteers to do it the upcoming Sunday, I have never had any takers. The force that keeps us seated and quiet during a sermon is but one of many faces of peer pressure. It exerts an irresistible pull on us. We are all subject to its influence. Without our being aware of its subtlety and omnipresence, it affects everything we do and everything we think. That is why we need to find a peer system for our children that carries out the values we want our kids to embrace as their very own. If we do not take an active, visible lead, our children will drift into their own peer system, which may not exert the kind of social influence we want.

Your child's peers will influence not only what he acts out (his behavior), but also what goes on in the innermost parts of his mind (his thinking and valuing). You need to be most aware of the mental effects of peer pressure.

In an article in the May 1991 edition of *Reader's Digest*, Kathleen McCoy wrote that parents are in the best position to help their kids resist troublesome urgings from peers. McCoy cited a study by Linda Grossman, a psychologist in Laguna Niguel, California, which found that kids who had worked with their parents on techniques to assert themselves in social settings were much less likely to take drugs two years later than those who had not.[3] Ms. McCoy's article listed the following ways that you can help your child beat peer pressure.

- Go one on one. Listen to your child when he talks to you. Give him as much undivided attention when he has something to say to you as you give your friends. Your child deserves no less. His peers listen to what he says and how he feels. You need to work hard against this kind of competition. Nothing will give him a greater sense of self-importance than feeling he is special to his parents.

- Help her face her fears. Talk to her about not being one of the herd. Share with her times when you found it hard to go against the crowd. Ask her if her friends would really quit liking her if she refused to do what "everybody's doing." Most people, including the young, generally admire someone who shows the moral courage to be different as long as the person is not weird in every other way.

- Help him to practice resisting peer pressure. Role-play with your child situations where someone is offering him a cigarette or alcohol or a drug. One program created by Grossman helps parents and teens role-play situations where they go from a simple "No, thanks" response to peer pressure to an emphatic "No, I don't want to do that" and on to a self-confident "I don't need that stuff, and I don't need to be like everyone else." They also learn tactics such as ignoring the other person, leaving the scene, and threatening to tell parents, teachers, or even the police.

- Bolster your child's self-respect. When was the last time you asked your child's opinion about a subject? Maybe you never have. Perhaps you should start. If you value your child's thoughts, being careful not to ridicule her but rather to guide her in adapting and respecting the morals and principles you hold, you will create the sense of belonging your child needs. One way to bolster self-respect is to develop a talent or a hobby and become involved in groups related to that interest. Children and youths who are busy doing things they enjoy with people who are going the same direction seldom have time for or interest in using drugs. It is important that your child choose the activity herself. You may have to experiment with several areas before she finds one she can grab onto and develop.

- Talk up positive peers and role models. Don't say, "Now, why can't you be like Johnny Jones? He really makes his parents proud of him." It is better to expose your children to people they can respect. This is where healthy role models can exert the greatest influence. Talk up the actions of people in your own neighborhood that you and your family can emulate. Talk down the *actions* (not the people) of those who have a disregard for the general well-being of society.

Young people are very impressed by media-hyped actors,

singers, and sports personalities. They want to relate to these heroes. They are not able to distinguish between the actor as a person and the role the actor is portraying. Heavy exposure to movies that glamorize petulant adolescence, self-indulgence, laid-back indifference, poutiness, sauciness, etc., make lasting impressions on children. The hot-blooded gladiator (Sylvester Stallone), cool-tempered terminator (Arnold Schwarzenegger), and cold-blooded exterminator (Charles Bronson) are not positive role models. These fictional characters excite the young into believing that it is all right to be violent, that they can also be big, bad, and resistant to anyone and anything. These "heroes" also make a child believe that it is cool to be aberrant.

• Discipline and intervene in your child's life with love. Oftentimes a child is not equipped with the kind of strength it takes to say no, so she lets someone influence her into doing something she does not want to do. This is where discipline comes in. Even though your young teenager argues that she can take care of herself at an unsupervised teenage party, hold tight. Explain that you love her and do not want to see her hurt

Family neglect. When anyone speaks about a child who is neglected, we usually think of one who is not properly fed, clothed, sheltered, or supervised. Physical neglect is a very common kind of neglect. Many children, especially in the inner cities, are not given proper physical attention. These children are fair game for gangs and drug dealers. However, neglect also appears in middle and upper class neighborhoods. For example, in 1979, the American Public Health Association said that "over-consumption malnutrition" from eating too much junk food would be one of the most significant health problems facing America's adolescents in the future. Children and teenagers who do not get enough nutrients in their food have problems in learning, relating to others, and behavior.

In this day when both parents work, or in single-parent homes where the mother or father must work, the preparation of nutritious food is the area that has suffered most. Children are often driven to school by a parent who first stops at Winchell's to pick up donuts for the kids' breakfast. Even though a sack lunch accompanies the child, the thing he eats first—and maybe the only thing he eats—is the dessert or sugar-juice drink. That night Mom may be too tired to cook, so the family sends out for pizza. Allowing bad eating habits in children is a form of neglect.

Ignoring emotional needs and not providing adequate supervision is another form of neglect. Parents are often too tired or too wrapped up in their own needs and activities to give emotional and physical attention to their children. When someone offers these lonely children a way to feel better, they take it. Often this way is through drugs.

I (McDill) once had a wealthy pair of Westlake Village parents come into family therapy over a problem they were having with their kids' acting out. They listed all the goodies (indulgences) they had given their kids and genuinely couldn't figure out why their kids were out of control. In the course of treatment, the parents were building their dream home in the most exclusive section of town and well into construction they suddenly realized—when the daughter asked where her room was—they had forgotten to plan their daughter's room into the home. "Oh well . . ." shrugged the father, "We can't go back now, it'll cost too much to rejigger the plans, she can make do somewhere else." Building went on, and yes, the daughter did make do somewhere else, in a string of chemical dependency and eating disorder hospitalizations. The daughter is still acting out.

Profile of a Drug-Free Child

In the following profile of a child least likely to use drugs, notice how many factors have to do with parental concern:

- Child comes from a strong family.

- Family has a clearly stated policy toward drug use.

- Child has strong religious convictions.

- Child is an independent thinker, not easily swayed by peer pressure.

- Parents know the child's friends and the friends' parents.

- Child often invites friends into the house and their behavior is open, not secretive.

- Child is busy, productive, and pursues many interests.

- Child has a good, secure feeling of self.

- Parents are comfortable with their own use of alcohol, prescription drugs and pills, set a good example in using these, and are comfortable in discussing their use.

- Parents set a good example in handling crisis situations.[4]

While the foregoing seem obvious, examinations have proven that drug abusers never received the kind of support described above. Assuring that your children are reared in this kind of an atmosphere will not necessarily protect them from drug abuse, but it will give them the props they need to learn to "just say no" to drugs.

What Works

1. Most drug problems occur because parents are not much involved in their kids' lives. Find out what the schools are teaching and reinforce it in our home. Don't leave drug education to the schools; show us you care by giving us your input.

2. Teach us what drugs can do to us physically and mentally.

3. If we children get into drugs, don't pretend to understand or think you understand what an addicted person goes through. Get professional help for us.

8

Sexual Involvement

The teen years begin with a bang: painful self-consciousness, social, psychological, and physical awkwardness; and a keen awareness of sexual differences and how such differences attract. Young men's voices crack, facial hair turns to beards, they learn about wet dreams and listen to their peers describe varieties of masturbatory experiences. They die a little every time they have to shower in the locker room if their manliness has not reached its full development.

Girls become obsessed with their breasts—they either develop too fast or not fast enough and they also blush with humiliation when they shower in phys-ed class. Menstruation becomes a fascinating and longed-for event.

Both boys and girls curse pimples that pop out overnight, hate the birdcage braces wrapped around their teeth, and seem compelled by some inner force to glance surreptitiously in every mirror or other reflection they happen to pass, cringing if even a hair is out of place. They fall in and out of puppy love, learn all about jealousy and insecurity, and try on many identities, some of which make parental skin crawl. It is all very normal, leading eventually to meaningful, uninhibited, free, playful, mature, and healthy adult identity and sexuality.

Gradually and finally, by the time young people are about eighteen, their identity comes together like a giant jigsaw puzzle, piece by piece until a picture forms—more or less.

Girls learn all about emotional intimacy first among their own sex, then with the opposite. Guys learn to be rough, tough he-men first, then gentle and tender much later. Girls learn all about trust and heterosexual security from the way their fathers treat them; guys learn tenderness, gentleness, and gentlemanliness from the way their fathers conduct themselves with and toward their mothers. A father's modeling role is paramount in child rearing. A mother's role is just as important.

In the United States, nearly five hundred babies are born each day to young women under eighteen. Of the more than a million American teenagers—one in ten—that become pregnant each year, thirty thousand are under fifteen. Nearly 40 percent obtain abortions.[1]

The Center for Disease Control (CDC) counted more than fourteen hundred cases of AIDS among teenagers, 1 percent of the total cases in the United States; however, the number of cases doubles every fourteen months. Since 1985, the syphilis rate for teens has jumped 67 percent.[2] If that isn't enough to scare a parent to death, consider the following: AIDS, syphilis, and gonorrhea—the most commonly discussed sexually transmitted diseases (STDs)—are not the only ones victimizing teenagers. The more common infections are chlamydia and genital warts, which are at record levels among teens.

Chlamydia poses a greater threat to teenagers than any other STD. The disease often has no overt symptoms. Those symptoms that do show up — abdominal pain, nausea, and low fever in women, and a discharge from the penis or painful urination in men—are often confused with other conditions so that treatment is delayed. Yet, if left untreated, chlamydia can cause sterility in both girls and boys.

Genital warts, small growths on the vulva, vagina, cervix, anus, penis, and urethra, have no permanent cure. Even though warts are removed, at least 20 percent grow back. As many as one-third of all sexually active teens have genital warts. If the warts continue to grow they may eventually block body openings.[3]

Further statistics from CDC indicate that more than 51 percent of girls between fifteen to nineteen engaged in premarital sex in 1988, almost double the 28.6 percent reported in 1970. The greatest increase in sexual activity is among middle-class, white, heterosexual kids.[4]

Dr. Lillian Rubin, professor of sociology at Queens College in New York City and a senior research associate at the Institute for the Study of Social Change at the University of California, in her book *Erotic Wars*, told of a 1987 study of thirteen- and fourteen-year-old children from three rural Maryland counties. Of these, 58 percent of the boys and 47 percent of the girls had had sexual intercourse. She also cited a study of young, active church members at eight conservative Christian evangelical denominations in the Midwest and South. Forty-three percent of those surveyed had had intercourse by the age of eighteen.[5]

When we speak about children being *safety-smart* regarding sexuality, there are three areas they need guidance in. The first is sexual experimentation ("Fooling Around"); next is sexual abuse ("Being Exploited"); third is homosexual inclination ("What Am I?").

Fooling Around

During the Victorian Era, anything that fell under the broad category of *sex* was firmly cloaked in euphemism, safely hidden under the covers, tightly lidded down as if it were something shameful. Since the sexual revolution of the sixties, however, and even before that time, SEX has burst into the open. Not only have promiscuity, sexual adventurism, and deviance come out of the closet, they play on the front lawn.

"Nobody these days lobbies for abstinence, virginity, or single lifetime sexual partners. That would be boring," wrote Robert C. Noble, professor of medicine at the University of Kentucky College of Medicine.[6] This article was written as a response to the idea of providing free condoms to high-school students in an attempt to slow down the spread of AIDS. Dr. Noble, an infectious diseases physician and an AIDS doctor, said there is no such thing as "safe sex." He quoted from a recently published government report, "Abstinence and sexual intercourse with one mutually faithful uninfected partner are the only totally effective prevention strategies."[7]

The stuffy, hypocritical, and misguided principles of the Victorian Era were an over-reaction to the ideals of Judeo–Christianity. It was a time when proper young ladies were never alone with young men until the day of their marriage. Ned Zeman wrote:

> Today's courtiers get busy in the fifth grade. In one Oakland, California, grade school the first-kiss process goes like this: two ten-year-olds, chaperoned by a four-foot-tall (but no doubt mature beyond his years) "witness," descend to the school parking lot under a cloak of danger and intrigue almost unfathomable to the rest of us. The next thing the world knows, the witness is careening into the lunchroom and hollering, as only an overwrought prepubescent can: "They did it! They did it! They're *going!*"[8]

This "first-kiss" episode used to take place later in life than elementary school age. But today the idea that "everybody's doing it," stimulated by pop music and violent sadistic Madonna–esque films, has an appeal to younger and younger children, leading to more serious experimentation in "making love." The consequences of casual sex are evident in the areas of health, pregnancy, abortion, and lost dreams and ideals.

Many Third-World countries solve the problem of raging sexual urgings in young people by encouraging early marriages. Girls as young as twelve and thirteen are given in marriage by their parents. However, so-called progressive cultures encourage young people to wait for marriage until they finish school and are well on their way to a profession.

How do today's parents deal with the uncontrolled sexual practices of children and youths? Most educators, psychologists, and religious leaders say the biggest deterrent to acting out sexual activity in young people is warm, enveloping affection, and it begins with parental affection. Dr. Joyce Brothers wrote that "many teens act like psychologists to each other because they have no adult supervision or parents laying down the rules." She states that teenage girls are "so hungry for love" that they become "pushier in their behavior in order to get the attention of boys." Dr. Brothers feels that girls are so affection-starved that they cuddle and kiss and give in to sex as a trade-off for sincere concern and affection they should be getting from parents and family. She continued, "Both boys and girls want reassurances and attention, but often they don't know how to go about getting it. They think it would be uncool to ask for it."[9]

Another reason why children at younger ages are experimenting with sex is because they get their education in the wrong places. Thirteen-year-old Jennie is left alone during the day in the summertime. Her mother works, and Jennie is "too old for a babysitter." She entertains herself by watching soap operas. Then she gets together with her girlfriends and compares notes about the sex scenes she has observed. "I know everything about sex," she says. "When I'm ready I'll know exactly how to do it." Even though she thinks she knows how to perform, she is not ready for the emotional and physical consequences of sex. Her education is woefully incomplete.[10]

Sex education should begin in the home. However, tragically, few parents take the time or interest to explain to a child what he or she needs to know. Therefore, their silence allows their kids' peers, society, TV, movies, and videos to take over their job. On daytime soap operas, beautiful men and women hop in and out of bed several times during one episode. That's sex education, too.

Part of the confusion parents feel stems from the fact that in society at large there is no longer an agreed upon standard for what is morally right. Being a virgin no longer carries the importance it did thirty—even twenty—years ago. Couples marry later, often after having lived together. And pregnant teenage girls, once banned from school, are now allowed, if not encouraged, to stay and graduate with their classmates.

Parents who either do not know how to approach their kids with the subject of sex, or can never seem to find the "right time," hope the public school system is doing the job for them. Yet when the school system proposes sex education courses, some parents argue that giving children facts about sex will stimulate sexual interest and, therefore, activity. However, the implementation of sex education courses— or even the discussion of which curriculum or whether to offer sex education in schools at all—usually comes too late to be effective. Many children and youths are thinking and talking about having sex, even planning on it, before parents or educators ever make up their minds about discussing the matter.

Openly and honestly discussing sexuality with your child can enrich your relationship and reinforce your family's agreed upon values. It can open up avenues of communication that your child desperately needs and seeks. A child who understands where his parents stand on such a life-influencing issue will have a stronger base on which to build his own values for his teen years and to prepare for marriage and his own family life. He will better understand the consequences of irresponsible behavior.

Kathleen McCoy, co-author of *The New Teenage Body Book*, writes:

> Parents who choose to remain silent aren't doing their kids any favors. Teenagers will continue to pick up messages about sex from TV, music videos, movies, and their friends. But studies do show that teenagers who feel they can talk with their parents openly and honestly about sexual feelings and peer pressure are more likely to postpone sex.[11]

Being Exploited

The idea that children may be victims of sexual abuse while their parents are at work is a possibility no parent wants to consider. Yet, children are abused every day. Statistics indicate that one child out of every five has been sexually abused.[12] Most of these are victims of older siblings.[13] Many are abused by adult relatives or close friends. Some are abused by their own parents (usually stepparents), or the mother's boyfriends.

While many schoolteachers and authorities are trained in how to recognize a child who is being sexually abused, few parents would know what to look for or how to question a child about it. They feel that if they do not mention it, their child will be okay. The National Committee for Prevention of Child Abuse gives the following signs of sexual abuse. The child:

- has difficulty walking or sitting.

- suddenly refuses to change for gym or participate in physical activities (or becomes more modest in his or her home).

- demonstrates bizarre, sophisticated, or unusual sexual knowledge or behavior.

- becomes pregnant or contracts a venereal disease (particularly if under age fourteen).

- runs away.[14]

Children who are sexually abused are almost always threatened by their abuser with severe punishment if they tell anyone what is going on. Oftentimes, the sex abuser tells the child he will hurt the parents. This kind of threat prevents a child from telling about the horror and pain he or she is suffering.

Personal guilt, a feeling that the reason they are being treated in such a shameful way "must be my fault," is also a factor. Even though young victims of incest or molestation are innocent in the situation, they often feel that they have somehow brought it upon themselves, or their molesters manipulatively tell them it was their fault and they believe it and take on the blame.

Ninety-seven percent of those who were sexually abused as children will never report the incident.[15] Yet, sexual abuse can be very destructive. The immediate results can be scarred vaginas, rectums, and mouths, and sexually transmitted diseases. Long-term effects are even more devastating.

Shayla Lever gives several "shoulds" concerning protecting a child against sexual abuse.

- Children should understand their value, worth, and uniqueness. A child must believe she (or he) is worth defending before she can defend herself. A child who is unsure, timid, weak, or defenseless is vulnerable. A child who believes that she is as good and important as anyone else can begin to protect herself. Building good self-esteem in your child is more important than any other lesson your child can learn.

- Children should understand the importance of communication (talking) as the best way to tell others what they are experiencing and how they feel. An abuser will intimidate, threaten, and create fear in his victim to keep him from telling what is happening. A child whose parents believe that "children should be seen and not heard," or who is always made to feel that what he has to say is not important, will never learn to express his own feelings, fears, thoughts, or experiences. Every day, parents should take time to talk *with* their children, not *to* them. They should listen to childish chatter and try to sense any underlying fears or anxieties.

- Children should understand that feelings are a part of what makes people special and that they are just as important as any other part of them. Everyone has a right to feel, whether anger, happiness, fear, or sadness. Feelings are normal and healthy, and children should learn to deal with them, identify them, and talk about them—and the people who make them feel as they do.

- Children should know what "privacy" and "private parts" mean, and why they need special protection. They need to understand the concept of abuse and know what it means to be treated badly. Since children are being sexually molested at very early ages (even preschool age), many people believe they should be made aware of the danger to them and taught that they have options. A parent will tell a child not to run with a lollipop in his mouth, not to poke beans in his nose, or wave a stick or knife in another child's face. Just so, parents should explain about protecting his "private parts." Eyes, ears, noses, mouths all have names; so do breasts, buttocks, penises, and vaginas. Explaining that these parts need to be protected should be done in the same manner.

Parents must use the proper names for body parts, or in the case of a very young child, saying that all the parts that are covered by a bathing suit need to be protected. A child should understand that all parts of her body are her own possession. No one has the right to touch, bother, or hurt any part of her body.

• Children should understand the concept of "appropriate touch." Telling children what is a "good" touch and what is a "bad" touch is a good start, but more is needed. It is better to tell them who can touch them and under what circumstances. A caress can be a comforting response from a grandparent, but it could be a form of seduction from a molester. Some touches feel good, some hurt, some feel funny, some are wanted, some are unwanted. When your children are taught that their bodies are their own property and that even their siblings have no right to trespass on their bodies with hitting, biting, or kicking, it is easier to explain who has a right to touch them. Children should be assured that no one has a right to uncover any parts of their body and touch them.

• Children should understand the "say no" rule on two levels— externally *saying* "no" means "no"; internally *thinking* "no" means "I have value." If a child is taught that she is a unique, special, important, and valued person who has a right to expect good treatment, she will think "no" when she is being abused in any way—whether it is physical, sexual, or emotional. People who have survived prisoner-of-war camps say that this is one reason for their survival—they did not feel they deserved to be treated badly. When the child can think "no" and mean it, then she can verbalize a firm "no." Of course, if the molester is an older relative, he may not be turned away by a child's refusal to cooperate. A child should still learn to say no to *anyone* who might hurt or frighten her. If she cannot verbalize it, she will still survive the emotional effects if she has said no internally.

- Children should understand the "get away" rule. When a child is taught that she has a right to protection and safety, she should also be taught that she should get away from the source of danger as soon as possible. Many times, however, a child cannot get away from the abuse that is occurring at that moment. She needs to know that it is not her fault if she cannot run from the danger.

- Children should know the "tell someone" rule and should understand the difference between telling and tattling. The only way a parent can help a child who is being abused is if the parent knows what is happening. Most parents discourage tattling. So, often a child may begin to tell what her brother or brother's friends, or mother's boyfriend did, only to be shut up by mother saying, "What have I told you about being a tattle-tale?" What is the difference between "telling" and "tattling"? A child can be taught that "telling" is sharing something that may *protect* someone, while "tattling" is done solely *to get someone in trouble.*

- Children should be able to differentiate between good and bad secrets. When an abuser swears the child to secrecy, he sets up the child to be an unwilling co-conspirator who begins to feel dirty and guilty. A child who believes that she is valued, has rights, and will be listened to, may be more able to share an unhealthy secret than a child who has never had such teaching. Explain to your children that good secrets feel happy or exciting. They are about fun things, such as a surprise party. A bad secret feels scary, sad, or confusing. They are about bad things such as stealing, removing clothes, etc. They hide something. Bad secrets should be told. Assure your child that it is all right if he makes a mistake and tells a good secret. Better to give away a good secret than to hold back on a bad one.

- Children should know that if they are hurt or scared by bigger or older persons, it is *not their fault.* Our society tends to condemn the victim along with the perpetrator. Our laws seem to protect the guilty more than the innocent. Children sense this and will take the blame when they are abused. They need to be taught that no matter what the circumstances, no one deserves to be treated badly. If they forget the "say no" and "get away" rules, and no matter what their abuser tells them, they are not to blame.

- Children should understand the concept of bribery, the most successful method used to convince a child to engage in sexual conduct. The bribe may be a gift such as money, a puppy, or a bicycle, or it may be an emotional incentive such as friendship and love. Therefore, a child should be taught that if someone older or bigger tells him he can have the gift "If you do *this,*" anything that feels wrong, scary, or confusing, he should refuse, or at least say, "I'll think about it." Someone who really loves him would never ask him to do something unacceptable, dangerous, or something that should be kept secret.[16]

If you discover that your child has been abused, it may be necessary for him or her to receive counseling to overcome feelings of guilt, anger, and fear. These emotions stay deeply buried, sometimes for years, building and releasing their poison in seemingly unrelated ways.

What Am I?

Thirteen-year-old best friends Stan and Jim were upper-middle-class kids who satisfied their biological curiosity by hovering over the pages of *Playboy, Penthouse, Oui,* and other soft- and hard-core pornographic magazines. Of course, they experienced sexual arousal, and there was no way to satisfy the feeling except through masturbation.

Jim fantasized about the females on the magazine pages, and he was full of expectations as to how wonderful it was all going to be when he had a real woman in his arms, not just a fantasy. He was secure and confident about his ability to carry it all off without a hitch when circumstances provided the opportunity for sexual activity. Stan, though, was insecure, shy, and confused about his developing sexual self. He did not have such a clear idea about how he would do in the real sexual world when "it" actually happened, even though he and Jim fantasized about it zillions of times.

Once the boys got so aroused they decided to make believe the other was a person of the opposite sex. They got physical. In his mind's eye Jim saw Stan as that siren on the page before him. And to Stan, Jim was his female fantasy come true (anything is possible in one's imagination). Before long, he was getting aroused by Jim and no longer needed the female fantasy that had captured him before.

Jim went on, transferring his activities from Stan to "real" girls, while Stan, in his shyness and insecurity, was happy to continue his relationship with Jim. The moments he spent with Jim were special. He was safe with Jim. They bonded. However, to Jim these moments with Stan were developmental and soon passed. And he moved on without a moment's thought or hesitation to become physically active with appropriate partners—girls. Stan remained behind though, developmentally stuck in a sexual world few understand and even fewer accept.

While the pathways into sexual disorder are many, and vary from person to person, there is one subtle trap that springs without the person being aware of what is happening until it is very late in the game. That pathway is early teenage viewing of sexually explicit pornography. Young people who become sexually stimulated way too early by reading and looking at pictures or videos of explicit sexual activity, and who have no appropriate heterosexual outlet for their normal sexual urges, tend to turn to each other for an outlet. Rather than drifting into and out of homosexual play, which for many males and some females is common and has nothing at all to do with true homosexuality, some males get seduced and confirmed into the homosexual world.

Pornographic books, magazines, and videos cannot properly be blamed for all forms of criminal and deviate sexual behavior. But ill-timed stimulation of developing sexuality in preteen and teenage young people can negatively affect them for their entire lives. Homosexuality is one form of this negative effect.

Tom grew up a latchkey kid. Both parents were employed, and Tom had plenty of unsupervised time. When he was thirteen, he was visiting his friend Pete, fourteen. The boys found a cache of *Playboy* and *Penthouse* magazines and XXX-rated videos. They weren't well hidden, so Pete's dad must not have been too concerned about anyone's discovering them. Sure enough, boys being boys, they devoured the stacks of magazines with nudes and centerfolds. Their bodies, being wired neurologically correctly, went into instant hot circuit. But there was nowhere to turn for sexual release except masturbation. After that became routine, they masturbated each other. It seemed more exciting, more forbidden. Then they moved on to oral sex on each other, taking lessons from the XXX-rated videos. Boy! They were really into big-time sex now. When they took turns trying anal insertion—modeled in the videos— they knew they could not turn back or let go. They had a secret life with each other, and retreating into the father's den with its treasures got to be their primary mode of sexual release.

After several years they were still at it because it was familiar, comfortable, and exciting. While both of them had begun with intense sexual arousal to female nudes, they gave up the thought of sex with females as too risky. Sex with each other was safe, a no-risk proposition. When he was in his mid-twenties, Tom was referred to my (McDill) counseling practice by probation services. He had been caught in sexual involvement with other adolescent males.

Tom has never related sexually with a woman, and his ideas of what sexual sharing is all about will take considerable effort to rearrange.

Becoming saturated with pornographic material is only one avenue that can lead a young person to sexual disorder as a way of life. Many times, an older homosexual mentor guides a confused and lonely young teen into the world of homosexuality. Such a guide takes a naive, inexperienced kid by the hand and ushers him into a world of confusing pathology.

Roz was ten years older than thirteen-year-old Lynn, and Lynn thought she was really cool. Roz had been a family friend since she was a teenager. When Roz invited Lynn to join her on a trip, Lynn was flattered and excited by the invitation. Lynn's parents trusted Roz and saw no problem with the two girls heading out for a few days to visit some of Roz's old family friends, doing girl things.

Off they went in Roz's car. Lynn trusted her and attached no significance at all to Roz's gestures of friendship—like hugs and kisses, even on the lips. Soon, though, without knowing exactly why, Lynn felt Roz cross the line. Intuiting Lynn's discomfort, Roz began to talk about friendship and love and how to express these emotions. Lynn suspended her misgivings and gave in to Roz's physical expressions of love.

Physical cuddling, lingering touches, and kisses led to love-making, and Lynn did not put on the brakes. She was aroused and felt open and affectionate. Roz was careful to surround each step with a positive and nonthreatening context.

That trip with Roz was Lynn's introduction to sexual love between women. Lynn had been sheltered, had never discussed this kind of sexual relationship with her parents, and was sure such expressions were appropriate. Her father, a respected church elder, thought he had instilled solid Christian standards into his daughter. Who would think some woman would come into that context and seduce a naive young teenager?

Marilee, Heather's English Lit teacher, saw an innocence and freshness in Heather that was compelling. When the class read D. H. Lawrence's *Lady Chatterly's Lover*, Marilee and Heather had long discussions about Lawrence's ideas on physical love. Heather was extraordinarily naive and deferential to Marilee's views, and the two grew closer and closer as the semester wore on. Without being aware of what was happening, Heather was drawn by Marilee's charisma, and her guard was down for what began to unfold between them.

Hugs began innocently enough soon lingered beyond what was normal for mere friendliness. Kisses on cheeks became kisses on lips. Feelings intensified into passion for Marilee and a confusing adolescent crush for Heather, who was too embarrassed to discuss it with anyone. Marilee convinced Heather that their love was special, clean, pure and even spiritual. She led Heather into a sexual love that confused and excited Heather. When the affair became public information and Marilee lost her teaching job and credentials, it took Heather a long time in therapy to sort through her feelings. The confusion and shame are still there; weaker, but still there.

A bewildering array of experiences during adolescence, combined with certain random happenings, and the guidance of people who are not concerned with their partners' best interests can cause teens to enter a world they did not create or choose, and which is entirely preventable. If they are more psychologically aware and sophisticated about lifestyles, young people can steer away from certain experiences at critical stages of development. They can be ready to say no earlier and more clearly, and the outcome can be far different from those described above.

Hurting adults often trace their homosexual selves back to a period of overwhelming confusion and loneliness when for some reason they felt cut off from people around them and a sympathetic adult homosexual friend took interest in them. Unless they are helped to remember how they came to take this pathway, they can honestly say that "homosexuals are born, not made." While this statement may serve to absolve them from responsibility for certain choices, it is not necessarily true. They were seduced into this "alternate lifestyle."

How can you as a parent help your children develop their sexuality?

- Become comfortable with talking about sex with your kids from the time of their first questions.

- Establish a good understanding of your own sexual self. Develop and maintain a happy sex life with your spouse and be openly physically affectionate with that partner. Let your kids know you have a good sex life with your spouse by openly hugging, kissing, and expressing affection toward your partner to your heart's content.

- Tell your kids about homosexuality early (and about other sexual disorders later) without deriding the homosexual (or any disordered person). All people deserve human decency and respect based on their character, apart from sexual orientation.

- Remember that knowledge and information are not what leads kids to early sexual experimentation or activity. Ignorance and naivete do. Kids should feel proud, not ashamed, that they are well-informed—preferably by their parents—about sexual matters. They should know that they do not have to prove to their peers that they are "with it" by "doing it," but by not doing it.

- Freely give your kids a lot of hugs, warm, all-enveloping affection, and genuine (not fawning or effusive) praise. That way they will not need to seek hugs and affirmation in all the wrong places, the wrong ways, and with the wrong people.

- Develop a personal value system and live it out, stick to it, and talk about it to your kids. Help them to understand while they are young why you have your particular value system. By the time they reach high school, you will not have to talk about it so much—just keep living it.

What Works

1. Be open with us from day one. Always be ready to answer questions. Be comfortable with using proper names for body parts, etc.

2. Give reasons why not to have premarital sex:
   teaches us the discipline needed for marriage; pregnancy; disease; our family's values system, a higher view of sex.

3. Be careful what we watch on TV and in movies.

4. Assure us that it is natural to be curious about sex and if we don't feel comfortable talking with you, give us the option of talking with other responsible adults.

5. Reserve the right to forbid us to date someone you don't trust. Instead, invite the date to do something with our family. We might be upset, but we'll know you love us.

6. Our parents have a good relationship with each other. Our fathers treat our mothers with love and respect. That is what we will look for in our own friends. If you teach us respect for each other when we are young, that respect will carry over into our dating years and marriage.

9

One of the Few

Lamar was new to the district. His dad, who was pretty high up at work—vice president of something—had been transferred to the new corporate headquarters, and the family had just bought a lovely, stately old home on "the bluffs."

Lamar was gentle, well-tutored, intelligent, refined, muscular, good-looking, and very athletic. On his first day at the local high school he had the first of many rude awakenings. In the area was a secret, blue-collar-level, white-pride youth gang that copied, with excitement and sickening exactness, the scare tactics of the South's oldest hate group—the Ku Klux Klan. There was also a Skinhead opposing gang that caused the school no end of grief with bigoted, hateful activities. And here was Lamar, one of a very few black students at a school that was 97 percent white, a symbol of everything both gangs hated, plopped in the midst of a sea of hatred.

Lamar realized he had better learn fast who his friends would be. Anti-black white males have a unique and indescribably obscene anger for black males and anyone who rises up to defend them. And Lamar knew that no white female could be a friend. These gang members would have special words for her—none of them printable.

Most of America probably believed that when the smoke from the violence of the civil rights movement finally cleared and the resulting laws brought about a nervous—and sometimes grudging—acceptance of the black members of our population, our racial problems would end. Not so! More than any time in history, the United States has admitted an enormous crowd of refugees from war-torn Asian and Arab nations and, from our own continent, Latin American refugees and job-seekers. The result is incredible racial tension. This is more graphic in larger cities. In one Southwestern high school there are forty-seven different ethnic and language groups—American Blacks and Chicanos, and children from Latin America, the Philippines, China, Taiwan, Japan, Vietnam, Cambodia, Laos, Thailand, Indonesia, Malaysia, Burma, India, Tibet, Pakistan, Iran, Iraq, Kuwait, and a host of other smaller nations.

When the people from this many countries settle into the same neighborhoods, not only do they often find animosity from White-Anglo-Saxon-Protestants (WASPs), but also animosity between each other. Jeffrey L. Munks, in an article in an edition of *National School Safety Center Newsjournal*, discovered this fact in an interview with

> a successful, well-educated and articulate Vietnamese businessman. We were discussing Southeast Asian refugee population trends in California. At one point, I asked him why so few Cambodians live in a particular California city that seemed almost dominated by Vietnamese. His response was unsettling: "Cambodians are dogs." He could see the shock on my face and followed quickly by saying, "It's the same with you. In America, you hate your blacks. . . . It is the same in my country. The Vietnamese hate the Cambodian. The Cambodian hate the Laotian. The Laotian hate the Hmong. And the Hmong hate everyone."[1]

When children from these various nations settle in America, not only do they have to cope with a culture that is extremely alien to them, they have to cope with age-old hatred from other ethnic groups.

This problem is not exclusive to large cities. It is the same all over America. Residents of many small towns resent *anyone* from outside coming into their communities to live, take their jobs, and increase their school enrollments. Resentment, fear of the unknown, and hatred multiply if the strangers are of another race or ethnic background that introduces unfamiliar cultures and religions. The result is bigotry. Bigotry is not something we are born with, it is something we learn and teach. Children are quick to pick up and play out these feelings.

In an attempt to fulfill the statement in the American Declaration of Independence that "all men are created equal, and that they are endowed by their Creator with certain inalienable rights, that among these are life, liberty, and the pursuit of happiness," federal laws have been enacted and enforced that were intended to provide a more equitable lifestyle for minorities. These include laws on integration which, in some areas, served only to increase interracial problems. Cultural and religious differences still kindle ethnic competition and pride. Also, these attempts at integration have slowed down the teaching process in some schools and forced teachers to learn a variety of new languages so that they can communicate with the children in their classes.

On the more positive side, the influx of other nationalities and cultures gives our children who are not globe-travelers the opportunity to learn more about their world and its peoples. Even young children are given a chance to become familiar with other cultures and to pick up words and phrases in languages they may otherwise never have been exposed to. If the situation can be seen as an opportunity rather than a problem, it can become a learning experience instead of a challenge to defend turf.

The overall consideration, however, is that we are now an irreversibly multicultural country. Families of other races and nationalities are here to stay. How we prepare our children for this fact can make a difference in the way they—foreign- and native-born—adapt to their environment.

Teach Your Children to Respect Other Groups and Cultures

Few parents would deliberately say, "I want my child to grow up believing that he is better than anyone else in the world. I want him to look on people of other races and cultures as inferior to himself. I want him to hate, abuse, and intimidate people who are not of his color or religion. We are better than anyone else because we are American whites, and I want my child to believe this. I don't care if it leads to warfare, murder, or his imprisonment." Yet, we parents do very little to prepare our children to see other people as having value and worth.

National and cultural pride is a good thing. It is important to feel good about our country, our roots, and our customs. Pride becomes negative when we feel that there is no room in our center of life for those from other countries and cultures, that our country and way of life are better than anyone else's. In generations past we read stories and verses to our little children that reflect this very attitude, such as Robert Louis Stevenson's "Foreign Children":

Little Indian, Sioux or Crow,
Little frosty Eskimo,
Little Turk or Japanee,
O! don't you wish that you were me?

You have seen the scarlet trees
And the lions over seas;
You have eaten ostrich eggs,
And turned the turtles off their legs.

Such a life is very fine,
But it's not so nice as mine:
You must often, as you trod,
Have wearied not to be abroad.

You have curious things to eat,
I am fed on proper meat;
You must dwell beyond the foam,
But I am safe and live at home.

Little Indian, Sioux or Crow,
Little frosty Eskimo,
Little Turk or Japanee,

O! don't you wish that you were me?[2]

Actually, people of the world—American Indian, Turk, and "Japanee"—all have pride in their own cultures. Comparatively few of them want to be Americans. What they do want are many of the same opportunities Americans are blessed with while still retaining their cultural traditions, heritage, and backgrounds.

Louise Derman-Sparks, a faculty member at Pacific Oaks College in Pasadena, California, heads a special project on anti-bias curriculum for the public schools. She says that "in a society where racism continues to prevail, it is insufficient, and highly unlikely, to be 'non-biased.' Nor is it sufficient to be an observer. Rather, it is necessary for each individual to actively intervene and counter the personal and institutional behaviors that perpetuate oppression."[3]

Strengthen Your Child's Sense of Personal Identity

The community of Mount Airy in northwest Philadelphia has a workable integration program. Due to the efforts of many of its citizens, blacks and non-blacks have learned to live peacefully, harmoniously, and happily side by side. In fact, as Jerry Buckley wrote in *U.S. News and World Report,* "Once a year, early in May, thousands gather for a community picnic that in most U.S. cities is a fantasy."[4] This harmony has been going on now for thirty years. However, it is something that has to be worked at continually.

Author Buckley told about two six-year-old friends—Phoebe, who is white, and Jennifer, who is black. The two girls "play together, sometimes pray together, and have come to see each other's grandmothers almost as their own."[5] But as they grow up, race is becoming a factor in their lives. One incident has to do with their hair. When Jennifer's mother, Donna, had her hair straightened, Jennifer also wanted straight hair "like Phoebe's." Donna realized that she was sending the wrong message to her daughter, that straight hair was better. She had her hair cut back to its usual style.

Phoebe's mother, Janet, has done her part to reassure Jennifer that she is beautiful, but the little girl has a hard time accepting her blackness. Sometimes when Jennifer goes with Phoebe and her family on outings, Jennifer worries that people may think she is adopted. Jennifer's family and friends need to help her establish a strong sense of personal identity. Also, the local schools need to encourage every child's self-esteem and pride.

Louise Derman-Sparks outlines four goals that will help children develop these qualities.[6]

Goal 1: *Construct a knowledgeable, confident racial and ethnic identity. Race* refers to skin color and other specific physical characteristics of a group of people; *ethnic* has to do with the geographical place of family origin and the way of life associated with the group. Ms. Derman-Sparks suggests that parents and child-care agencies begin fostering a positive racial identity before children enter school. They could provide pictures, books, and dolls that show a range of skin colors, eye shapes, and hair textures, explaining that the differences are not good or bad, they are just varieties of the same thing.

Children often "hate" things about themselves that have nothing to do with their race or ethnic background. Much of this is the result of Madison Avenue advertising and promotion of products that promise to make each of us into Barbie and Ken dolls. Children with straight hair want it to be curly; children with freckles wish they had flawless, tan skin. The skinny ones want to be more curvy, the fat ones want to look starved. They grieve over button noses, big ears, buck teeth, red hair—anything that someone else has that seems better. Self-acceptance is very important. Parents would be wise to minimize physical appearance and begin to concentrate on character, personality, ability, talent, and other admirable qualities every person has. When your child has a strong self-image he will not be so critical or envious of another child's appearance, color, eyes, hair, or accent.

Goal 2: *Develop knowledgeable, comfortable, empathetic understanding of cultural diversity. Culture* broadly describes the set of rules for behavior which different peoples adapt. These rules are an essential source of both individual and group identity. Parents should not try to obliterate their family's cultural background, but should study and understand the unique attributes every culture has. In many families there are two distinct cultural backgrounds that can be studied.

Sometimes we are ashamed of our family background. A publishing company executive expressed his embarrassment and shame over an aging aunt he cared for because she was from the Appalachian sector of the United States, a "mountain woman." Blacks who struggle out of the ghettos become ashamed of family who still live in the inner city. On the other hand, Americans who originated from English, French, Spanish, or Russian nobility are often tempted to flaunt their heritage.

How can parents help their children retain their cultural integrity and still feel comfortable and accepted in our larger society?

Again, Derman-Sparks emphasizes that parents carefully select stories and movies about children from different ethnic groups who have the same fears, emotions, dreams, hopes, and needs as your children have—stories that tell about common issues all young children face, such as the birth of a sibling. A new baby in a family sparks the same emotions in children of all races and cultures.

Teach children about the unjustified enslavement of people on the basis of their race or culture groups, such as the Africans brought to this country, or the Chinese who immigrated or were imported like chattel to the United States only to find themselves earning meager (if any) wages building the railway system. Even in this decade we read about Latin Americans who are brought into the United States and sadly made to work as slave labor.

Teach older children to identify the important cultural rules, values, and beliefs in your own ethnic group and how your family reflects these in your lifestyle—what you eat, where you worship, and often what you wear or refuse to wear. Call attention to your child's friends who have different cultural backgrounds. Invite them over to share your way of life and explain why you do what you do.

Encourage your children to be open to their friends' choice of food, worship, clothes, and personal habits that are culturally inspired. They should be aware that this nation was established by people of diverse cultures and that it has become strong because of this fact. Acceptance of diversity does not necessarily mean that children will adapt the cultural differences as their own lifestyle. How you live your own beliefs and customs will determine how your child will live his.

Goal 3: *Learn to think critically about racial bias.* Stereotyping, misinformation, and prejudice are manifestations of racial bias. Everyone in every neighborhood is exposed to racial biases. Many large cities have pockets of Irish, Puerto Ricans, Italians, Poles, Cubans, American Indians, Vietnamese, etc. Each of these mini-national groups tends to fiercely protect its culture. Sometimes, however, individuals—especially children—within these cultural groups begin to believe erroneous ideas about their own group. Such beliefs limit vision and cause misunderstanding, hurt, and conflict.

Weed out of your home any books, posters, greeting cards, songs, and jokes that are untrue, unfair, and hurt other people's feelings. Point out unfair stereotypes you see on television, in magazines, etc. and correct them. Talk critically about white supremacist groups, such as the Ku Klux Klan and the neo-Nazis, and how to combat their influence.

Goal 4: *Gain skills for challenging discriminatory behavior directed against oneself and others.* Before we can effectively challenge discrimination on the basis of race, ethnic, or cultural backgrounds we need to know non-violent conflict-resolution skills. And we need to be free of all bigotry and prejudice ourselves. Young children can learn about individuals and groups in their neighborhood who stand up for justice and act in ways that show every person to be equal and worthwhile.

Of course, it begins with you. Parents need to practice equality toward all peoples. Also, parents should see to it that their children's schools do their part to erase bigotry and racial discrimination. Teachers should never let a child reject another student because of race or ethnicity or call other children derogatory names that demean their race or culture.

Become Comfortable with Diversity

Even though Mount Airy has pretty well succeeded in becoming a model of integration, every once in a while prejudice rears its ugly head. Clinton Gibson is a successful businessman, the highest-ranking black at a financial institution in Philadelphia. One day he and his sixteen-year-old son were riding their bikes when a patrol car pulled up. The white officer asked, "Do you live around here?" Gibson pointed to a large brick home and replied, "Right in that house."

On the flip side, Karen Crist, a white librarian, was walking her dog near her house when an elderly black woman asked her, "Excuse me, miss, but have you lost your way?" The woman did not think a white person would live on that block.[7]

If you are at retirement age, you may still have a problem being comfortable around people of other races, religions, and cultures. America has not been working seriously at equality for a full generation yet. But our invitation, as it is expressed by Emma Lazarus's poem engraved on the Statue of Liberty, still stands: "Give me your tired, your poor, your huddled masses yearning to breathe free." This is an invitation to the people of the world who look to the "land of opportunity" as a place where they can have an equal chance to live happily ever after.

Think Critically About Bias

It is probably safe to say that most bias is learned. Whether or not they were aware of it, our parents taught us to be selective in our friends, and that selectivity often included rejection on the basis of color, religion, or culture.

Bias is also acquired because of personal experience. If you have ever been bested by a businessperson who happens to be Jewish you may tend to lump all Jews together as "sneaky" or "conniving." If you were ever mugged by a Black or a Chicano, you may develop a dislike of all African- and Latin-Americans. You would not, though, develop prejudice against the race of a person who mugged you if the mugger were of your own race.

Probably the most effective way of overcoming bias is to get to know individuals of other races, religions, and cultures. Teaching courtesy and modeling thoughtful behavior toward others is a positive model we can give our children.

Getting yourself and your family involved in the lives of a culturally or racially different family can open up interest in history, geography, world politics, and the humanities. It can inspire your children to learn the languages, songs, and dances of other peoples.

Research your biases. Try to find out why you have negative feelings about people who are different from you, then set about reorganizing your thinking patterns so you can begin to see people for what they are—different but equal.

Stand Up for Justice

If parents do not get involved in seeing to it that all people are treated justly, our cities will continue to be riddled with violence. Hate groups will still bomb and vandalize synagogues and mosques. Our "land of opportunity" will degenerate, and all of us will suffer the loss of our four freedoms as expressed by President Franklin D. Roosevelt, on the eve of our involvement in World War II:

> In the future days, which we seek to make secure, we look forward to a world founded upon four essential human freedoms. The first is freedom of speech and expression. . . . The second is freedom of every person to worship God in his own way. . . . The third is freedom from want. . . . The fourth is freedom from fear.[8]

One place all of us can fight bias is at the polls. We can vote for equality in schools, on jobs, in politics, in all areas of life. We can teach our children that every person has worth, regardless of his color, religion, clothing, food, or daily customs. We can instill in our children a strong sense of self-esteem so that even if they are one of the few they can still feel that they count, that they are needed, that they can contribute something good to their neighbors.

It is good to be reminded that, unless you are a pure Native American Indian, someone in your family was once one of a few, a minority in this country who came, as many still do, seeking opportunity, freedom, peace, and happiness.

What Works

1. Teach us to respect all people. Color should not be a part of deciding who our friends will be. If you have friends of different colors and cultures, we learn through your example.

2. Let's travel as much as we can to learn about various cultures. If we can't travel by plane, boat or train, let's travel by book—using our home libraries or library cards.

3. Be firm about the use of racial jokes and slurs in our home. Make sure you don't use them, make sure we don't use them, and don't allow others to say such things in our house.

10

The Law and School Safety

Every state has volumes of laws concerning mandatory schooling of children. They vary as to the required time a child must spend in formal education, but in all cases they state that education is more than a right, it is a requirement. Some states recognize independent or home study as an alternative to public or private school education. But whatever form it takes, children must attend a legally prescribed number of years in learning the three *Rs*.

There are also laws that guarantee your child's right to be safe in school. As a result of a court case known as *New Jersey v. T.L.O.*, 105 S. Ct. 733, 742 (1985), in which the Supreme Court upheld a reasonable search of a student's purse, the Court recognized that "maintaining order in the classroom has never been easy, but in recent years school disorder has often taken particularly ugly forms; drug use and violent crime in the schools have become major social problems."[1] Consider the following statistics:

- Nearly three million criminal incidents occur each year on school campuses.

- Every day, ten children are killed by handguns.

- It is believed that one hundred thousand children carry a gun to school each day.

- At least 25 percent of the nation's schools are vandalized every month.

- Schools are burglarized five times more often than are businesses.

- Break-ins, bomb threats or incidents, trespass cases, extortions, and thefts of school property are not always reported. One of every one hundred schools experiences a bomb-related offense in a typical month.

- Each month around three hundred thousand students are attacked in schools, with younger students being the most likely victims.

- Forty percent of robberies and 36 percent of assaults on teenagers occur in schools, with statistics even higher for youths twelve to fifteen years of age.

- More than two-and-a-half million secondary school students are victims of theft each month, many involving the use of force, weapons, or threats.

- Approximately one hundred and thirty thousand secondary teachers have something of value stolen each month.

- More than five thousand teachers are attacked every month, one thousand of them being seriously injured enough to require medical attention.[2]

In 1982, California voters added to their state constitution "The Victims' Bill of Rights." One section of this provision, entitled "Right to Safe Schools," states: "All students and staff of public primary, elementary, junior high, and senior high schools have the inalienable right to attend campuses which are safe, secure, and peaceful."[3] The responsibility for protecting our children's right to safe schools, however, cannot be left solely in the hands of school authorities, law enforcement officers, and politicians. Parents and other members of the business community must do their part in assuring the safety of teachers and children in schools.

How can you as a parent help? Teach your child acceptable moral behavior. Set the proper example. Monitor his reading and TV watching. Teach him to respect authority by being yourself respectful of authority, and then being truly respectable as an authority. Teach him by example to make wise choices. Support your school's rules and regulations. Become personally involved in your child's safety at school. Know and pursue your legal rights to have safe schools.

Teach Your Child Acceptable Moral Behavior

Socrates, in the fifth century B.C., said: "The children now love luxury; they have bad manners, contempt for authority; they show disrespect for elders and love to chatter in place of exercise. Children are now tyrants, not servants of their households. They contradict their parents, and tyrannize their teachers." It seems that nothing has changed in the past twenty-five centuries. However, there was a time when we espoused virtue and morality. In the well-known poem "If," Rudyard Kipling, the English author, gave this advice to boys:

> If you can keep your head when all about you
> Are losing theirs and blaming it on you, . . .
> If you can talk with crowds and keep your virtue,
> Or walk with Kings—nor lose the common touch, . . .
> Yours is the Earth and everything that's in it,
> And—which is more—you'll be a Man, my son![4]

Today, however, it seems that virtue, morality, honesty, and righteousness are considered old-fashioned. People are actually embarrassed to admit they have any of these characteristics. The Bible and Horatio Alger are "out." "If it feels good, do it" is "in." We manifest more emotion and make more noise about saving the redwoods than we do about saving our children from the devastation of moral bankruptcy. School children used to cut their teeth on *McGuffey's Eclectic Readers* that taught the Golden Rule and how to distinguish good from bad. Today they take the examples they see on TV and in movies as their role models.

However, grass roots Americans are beginning to long for the return of virtue and moral values. Parents are terrified of the appalling influences that are trying to snatch their children from them. Unfortunately, the media have not responded to this yearning. Movies and TV focus on action, excitement, titillation, sex, violence, drug-taking, and materialism. They claim that these things make money, but some of the greatest money-making movies have been those that exemplify goodness, such as *Mary Poppins.* So we must assume that the entertainment industry chooses to show these non-virtuous themes for other reasons.

It is up to parents to counteract the negative influences in our society. How?

Set the Example

Teaching your child from the time he is an infant what is good and what is bad will have greater impact than what he learns outside the home. However, the "do as I say, not as I do" philosophy will not cut it with your child. He will do as you *do,* even if you tell him not to.

Russel C. Hill, founder of the American Institute for Character Education, developed a list of fifteen basic values shared by world cultures: courage, conviction, generosity, kindness, helpfulness, honesty, honor, justice, tolerance, sound use of time and talents, freedom of choice, freedom of speech, good citizenship, the right to be an individual, and the right of equal opportunity. Your practicing and teaching these values will promote peace in your home, your schools, your community, and your nation.

Monitor What Your Child Reads and Watches on TV

In 1985, Attorney General Edwin Meese III appointed a commission to study the nature and extent of pornography. After fourteen months the panel published its results. The report included a list of 2,323 separate pornographic magazines, 725 book titles, and 2,370 films that graphically depict every form of sexual activity and perversion—including homosexual intercourse, sado-masochism, rape of women and children, and bestiality.[5] This material is no longer found only in "adult" bookstores, it is available from vending machines and your local video rental stores. Not only that, your children are able to "dial-a-porn" from your home.

Even if your child is not into hard-core pornography, a daily dose of soap operas or prime-time TV will expose him to more aberrant sexual behavior than his young mind is able to sort through. Children soak up values like a sponge. Parents need to exercise influence over their children's choices of reading material, movies, and TV.

Teach Respect for Authority

During the sixties, Americans began to lose their respect for authority; all authority figures came under question and even under fire. It was the age of flower children, hippies, sit-ins, demonstrations, marches, riots, love-ins and defiance of anything acceptable and authoritative. Some of these demonstrations were positive and resulted in breaking the status quo so that equality and freedom became more possible for all of our citizens. But much of the confrontation was caused by those who resented any person, law, or tradition that prevented them from doing what they wanted to do. The outcome was that Americans never regained that necessary respect for authority that exemplifies our definition of "civilization."

Parents are the first authorities children recognize—or don't recognize. Unless you teach your child to obey and respect your discipline, teachings, and values, he will never learn to respect his schoolteachers, the law, the authorities who enforce the law, or his country's leaders.

In his article "Teaching Morality," William Raspberry said: "A frightening number of young people . . . seem almost devoid of [natural] controls [of behavior]. They may refrain from certain actions out of fear that someone will make trouble for them, or call the police, or 'punch their lights out,' but not because of any self-imposed limits on their behavior."[6] Mr. Raspberry says that educators (and parents) "imagine that their students will soak up, as through osmosis, a clear sense of right and wrong and that, in any case, morality training is not their responsibility."[7]

Teach Children to Make Wise and Responsible Decisions

Freedom of choice is guaranteed by God and country. William J. Bennett, former U.S. Secretary of Education, wrote that "every choice has a consequence, and some consequences are better, healthier, and sounder than others. To refuse to discriminate between good choices and bad ones is to deny the distinction between a free society and an oppressed one."[8] Teaching children how to make choices that are "better, healthier, and sounder than others" is the responsibility of parents first, and church and school educators second.

Every day we are faced with making choices, from what to eat for breakfast, what to wear, what to do, to the more serious choices. Children are faced with that which will not only determine their future destinies but also sometimes whether or not they will have a future: Do I want to take this class or that one? Do I want to play baseball or do my homework? Do I want to ask Ginny to the dance or Lisa? Do I want to go to school today or ditch? Should I get the answers to tomorrow's test from Tom? Shall I buy some uppers from that kid who keeps asking me? Should I steal that video game I want or save up my allowance and buy it? Should I get Dad's gun and practice with it?

Some choices are not taught to children. They will soon let you know that they don't choose to like broccoli or brussels sprouts. She likes the red T-shirt better than the white one. He wants to be a fireman, not a businessman. A wise parent will see to it that his child has the freedom to choose for himself many of these things. A wise parent also knows that the same vitamins and minerals can be found in food other than broccoli or brussels sprouts. But most choices in life have to be taught.

Some choices are not negotiable. Parents will tell a small child that he must not go into the street or he will get hit by a car. He must not go swimming alone or he could drown. He must not drink anything out of a bottle that he finds under the sink.

Some choices are negotiable. These usually stem from family rules. Who takes out the garbage tonight? Whose turn is it to wash dishes? What time is curfew? A child who is given sufficient freedom to make choices that are negotiable will learn about the non-negotiable ones. When he is old enough to go to school, he is ready to learn about obeying the school rules, and later the laws of the nation.

Support Your School's Rules

The three *Fs* of school administration are to be Firm, Friendly, and Fair. Rules should be clearly communicated, consistently enforced, and fairly applied. Some rules set up by schools are essential to your child's safety and therefore are not negotiable: Students will not leave the school grounds during school hours without written permission from parents. Students will complete all assignments either in class or as homework. Students will be on time for all classes. Students are responsible for bringing their own pens, papers, books, and homework to school. No fighting is permitted on school grounds. Littering is not allowed. Smoking is not permitted on school property. These obvious rules should be respected.

Some not-so-obvious rules could be debated by children and parents. Things such as mode of dress, campus clubs, student government, parental involvement, textbook selection, teacher conduct, bilingual education, religious teaching at Christmas and Easter, and methods of enforcing discipline are all negotiable. Parents should participate in the setting of these school rules and then help uphold them. However, criticizing the school, its teachers, and the regulation in front of your children serves to teach them to disregard school authority and discipline. Parents will help their children become better citizens if they model and encourage obedience to the school's rules.

Become Personally Involved in School Safety

A "Checklist for Providing Safe Schools," directed at school authorities, appeared in the publication *School Crime and Violence: Victims' Rights.* If you feel your schools are not protecting your children the way they should, you can become involved in bringing about better conditions. Some of the things the schools in your community should do to provide safety are:

- Recognize that the duty to provide safe schools should be shared by (a) the school; (b) the student; (c) the parents; (d) your community.

- Assign specific responsibility for developing, implementing, and enforcing efforts to provide safe schools to an action team or other authority.

- Have an attorney knowledgeable in education law participate in the school's efforts to eliminate crime and violence.

- Determine how widespread school crime and violence are.

- Implement measures your group or organization can take to prevent crime and violence. For example, consider limiting access to school campuses by requiring school staff to challenge and assist outsiders. Set up volunteer parent supervision teams to monitor playgrounds, restrooms, lunch areas, and locker rooms. Remodel or add security aids such as improved lighting. Suggest if not create special education programs for students with behavioral disorders.

- Establish opportunities for students, parents, school staff, and community leaders to meet together to express comments, ideas, thoughts, suggestions, and concerns about school safety.[9]

Know Your Legal Rights to Safe Schools

If the schools in your community are not doing everything they can to assure safe schools, you can sue— especially if your child is injured or killed as a result of neglect by the school.

In "Victims Can Sue Bullies, Schools," author Donna Clontz wrote:

> Courts have ruled that school districts have a duty to warn students and to take reasonable precautions to protect students from foreseeable criminal acts. This responsibility derives from the special relationship schools have with students both to educate them and to control their behavior. Schools are expected to provide a thriving intellectual environment as well as one that is safe and welcoming. Although a school cannot ensure a student's safety, the school has a legal duty to properly supervise student activity in a reasonable and prudent manner. . . . If a court finds . . . that the [school] staff callously disregarded the students' constitutional rights to remain free from harm, a civil rights action also would be successful against the school and its staff.[10]

How does your school's safety climate compare with that in other schools? The following questions will help you determine your school's safety. Rate the factors in this way: 1 = strongly disagree; 2 = disagree; 3 = agree; 4 = strongly agree.

_____ 1. Our school has comparatively few discipline problems.

_____ 2. Vandalism is not a problem in our school.

_____ 3. Attendance is good in this school.

_____ 4. Student and staff morale is high.

_____ 5. Pupil achievement is high.

_____ 6. Pupils feel a high sense of ownership and pride in their school.

_____   7. The school staff and students trust, care about, and respect one another a great deal.

_____   8. The school's various social groups, or cliques, communicate well with one another, respect one another, and work together for the benefit of the school.

_____   9. Students and staff frequently participate in problem-solving and school-improvement activities.

_____   10. The threat level in our school is low (i.e., people do not have to worry about being treated disrespectfully, becoming failures, or being physically harmed).

_____   Total

A score under 20 indicates a very negative school climate; 20-25 is negative; 26-30 is positive; and about 30 is a very positive climate.[11]

What Works

1. Keep informed about our schools' rules and reinforce them at home. We appreciate consistency!

2. You can teach us to respect authority by your example. If you speak respectfully about teachers, principals, and staff—as well as police and government officials—we will too.

11

Your Part in Making Schools Safer

We parents tend to abdicate parenthood during the hours our children are under the responsibility of school authorities. Yet we are the most significant factor in their safety and success at school. Getting involved can improve our children's achievement, both academically and socially, because their safety and success are directly related to how much we care.

When parents become involved in their school's comprehensive improvement program, the welfare and achievement of their children are significantly and consistently improved. The kids show higher grades and test scores, better long-term academic achievement, more positive attitudes and behavior, and the school programs are more effective and successful.[1]

Unfortunately, few of us get personally involved in our children's schools. A study on parental involvement released by the Center for Research of Elementary and Middle Schools at Johns Hopkins University found that 70 percent of all parents never go to the school building in any volunteer capacity. No task is more important than raising a child, and no one is in a stronger or more effective position to provide for the education and safety of our children than parents.

If this is such an important issue, why is it that so few parents make the effort to get involved in their children's schools? There are a number of barriers that hinder parental involvement.

The first barrier is the change in family structure. Economic conditions often require that both parents work outside the home, leaving little time for personal attention to the children, let alone time to volunteer some service to their schools. As we pointed out in Chapter 2, one third of today's students are latchkey children, and most men, women, and children live in some form of step-relationship.

Another barrier is simply the challenge of being a parent. The three most difficult positions in life are being a teenager, being a parent of a teenager, and trying to teach a teenager. We are challenged with two of these at once. So, by working with other parents we often can positively influence one another's children.

A third barrier is the school's resistance to parental interference. Some teachers do not want to work with parents, and some school administrators feel that parents get in the way of educating their children the way the administrators want to do the job.

Parents sometimes feel isolated from their children's schools. Other parents lack the training or the orientation to assist in school, while still others are apathetic or insensitive to the need. Some parents are poor role models.

Attending their children's classrooms on parents' night is commendable, but it is not enough. At least a few moms and dads need to get more involved if all the children are to come through their school years without physical, emotional, or educational damage and destruction. And all parents can get involved in researching how safe their local schools are before the child goes off to school.

On the School Grounds

Teachers cannot teach and students cannot learn in an environment filled with violence, intimidation, and fear. The quality of the instruction your children receive is directly related to their safety, security, and the climate at school. Many parents can take part of a day each week or each month to volunteer on the school campus or in the schoolroom to eliminate or cut down on these interfering influences.

Parents can enhance natural supervision at school. Noncustodial parents, visitors, violent intruders, strangers, and drug dealers have easy and unrestrained access to many school campuses. Someone needs to be watching out for this type of danger. Since the first line of defense should be school administrators and teachers, parents should insist that appropriate safeguards are in place and that the teaching staff is trained and prepared to handle intruders, angry students, and even frustrated parents or guardians who may disrupt the educational process. This is a big task for school administrators to take on in addition to their job of teaching our children, especially when most states are cutting education budgets so that schools are forced to operate with smaller staffs. So the second line of defense should be parents who can volunteer to stand guard on the school grounds, in the restrooms, and halls before school, during recess and lunch, and after school to see that no unauthorized person gains entry. Parents are also needed to chaperone at school games, dances, and other school-sponsored activities. They can volunteer their homes as "safe houses" for the safe passage of children to and from school.

Both school personnel and volunteer parents should learn how to manage a crisis and know emergency procedures that will eliminate or minimize the effects of violent intruders. Children need training, too. Most schools drill staff and students in how to respond in the event of fire, earthquake, or violent storm, but only in the inner city are they taught how to respond to acts of violence on school grounds or in classrooms. Parents and teachers together should implement a program that will teach preschool and elementary children what to do when they are threatened by violence, or how to respond when strangers are on the school campus.

Parents should participate in and support drug-free schools. If your community does not have programs that encourage children to stay off drugs, get together with other parents, school officials, law enforcement agencies, and other professionals and start one.

Parents should support safety programs their schools initiate. They should work with law enforcement agencies, community leaders, and school officials in developing and implementing a safety program for each school district. When their children are involved, they should cooperate in resolving such matters as assaults on students and teachers, theft, vandalism, and other types of disruptive behavior—especially if their child is accused as a culprit. They should help to promote a positive campus climate by immediately contacting school administrators when any act of violence touches their children. They should keep a written record of all names, times, and circumstances of such incidents.

Parents should insist on competent school administrators. Schools are responsible for properly selecting, training, supervising, and, when necessary, removing incompetent teachers or other administrators from the school setting. When mismanagement occurs, school districts are subject to multimillion dollar lawsuits. Safeguards such as fingerprinting and background checks of prospective teachers must be in place to screen prior felons.

Parents can visit classrooms as resource persons. Parents who are writers, musicians, athletes, businessmen, actors, policemen, attorneys, ministers, astronauts, computer technicians, nurses or other professionals can make presentations on their fields of expertise. Such involvement can make a dramatic difference in creating a climate of exciting learning in the classroom. They can work with school and community officials to develop community training programs in how to counsel and serve troubled youth and to provide activity centers for young people.

Parents should work with schools on developing meaningful curriculum programs. A comprehensive curriculum that nurtures, challenges, develops, and identifies a child's strengths should be developed. Curriculum that encourages young people to drop "in" instead of "out," that goes beyond the three *Rs*, that teaches life skills, how to get along with others, and good citizenship —including rights and responsibilities—must be given a more significant role.

In the Community

Work with law enforcement agencies. Clever lawyers can often get drug traffickers, violent youth, vandals, and even sexual offenders very light prison sentences or even probation. Parental interference can go a long way toward ridding your community of people whose sole aim is the destruction of your children.

Encourage businesses to get involved in schools. Organizations such as Honeywell and IBM already provide release time for employees to assist, visit, or volunteer in schools. Business is already mandated to provide release time to support the criminal justice system through jury duty, and national defense through the National Guard release program. Why not support the educational system the same way? If each employee were allowed as little as one day a year to volunteer time to the educational process, this could have a dramatic effect. Businesses need to be convinced that they have a stake in the educational enterprise. When young people are not properly educated, our nation's capacity to compete economically with world markets is diminished. When young people are not properly supervised, the community's crime rate increases, and businesses suffer.

Business organizations should provide before- and after-school child care. If the company you work for has ten or more employees, it should allow for child-care needs. Employers who have tested a child-care program have discovered that employee efficiency improves, absenteeism decreases, and general morale is higher. In short, it is to a company's advantage to see to it that their employees' children are properly supervised during the work-day.

Mentor programs should be encouraged. Children need role models. First and foremost, caring and involved parents should be their mentors. But when they are unable or unwilling or unqualified to serve in this capacity, then a "surrogate somebody" should be available to every student—another parent, a coach, a teacher, a youth worker. This is especially critical for children from single-parent homes.

Communities should work with schools to provide extracurricular activities and programs. Children and youths who are considered "at-risk" especially need additional resources and programs outside the school system that will inspire, involve, and motivate them into positive activities.

The community should develop ways to recognize student achievement. Certain service organizations already offer scholarships and special recognition to students who excel in academics or sports. More could be done on a broader basis to include students who achieve in less spectacular ways. Everyone loves recognition, to be looked upon as special. Such recognition does not have to cost a lot of money.

The community should launch positive media campaigns that focus on parents. Recognizing all parents by focusing on their parental responsibilities and rewards will serve to give status to this important role. Such things as bumper stickers, posters, or billboards that proclaim "Be Proud to Be a Parent" or "Stronger Parenting Builds a Stronger America" could be financed by private business and service organizations.

Children are this nation's most precious resource. It is only proper that we invest our energies in them to ensure a strong, competitive, and more enlightened America. Schools, the one common ground through which every student must pass, have the great opportunity to be the primary social agency that intervenes in the lives of all youngsters. In this sense, the school is an extended family, a concept captured most effectively by George McKenna, former principal of George Washington High School in Los Angeles, whose slogan is "We Are Family."

We must create a social revolution that restores the value of parenting and quality education, that recognizes potential in children, and that underscores the necessity of working together. If we wreck a car it can be discarded and replaced. But if we wreck a child, that precious resource is gone forever. The safety, security, and education of our children are the most important tasks we can undertake. We must begin to act now, because our children simply cannot wait. America's future depends on it.

What Works

1. Get involved in our schools. Visit our classrooms. Talk to us about what goes on whenever there is no teacher around.

2. Attend school games.

3. Before signing us up for a certain school, drive around it to see if the neighborhood looks safe. Pay attention to people who "hang around" schools.

4. Talk to school authorities and see what problems they are having that could lead to an unsafe school.

5. Talk to police and see if they have been called out to take care of a "problem" around school.

PART III

The Road Between

12

Abduction

Hundreds of thousands of children disappear each year. Of these, the vast majority (about 450,000) are runaways; between three and five thousand are abducted by either a parent or representative relative or a stranger.[1]

Parental Abduction

Parental abduction results when one parent in a divorce case is dissatisfied with the mediator- or court-imposed child custody decisions. A father may fear that his ex-wife will poison his child's mind against him, or that she may want to withhold his visitation rights, or she may remarry and move away from the area. A mother may fear that the child will be abused physically or sexually by the father. Whatever the reason, a parent who steals a child away from the other parent does more harm to the child than to the estranged spouse.

About half of all marriages in the United States end in divorce. Many divorced families reach an agreeable arrangement regarding the children's support and visitation rights, but 10 to 15 percent contest custody, visitation rights, and child support decisions.[2] Even if a child is not abducted, sooner or later all children of divorce will experience emotional upheaval to some degree as a result of the divorce, especially if there is ongoing unpleasantness over custody and care. Occasionally the battle results in the child being stolen from the custodial parent.

A CBS special presentation, "America's Missing Children," narrated by the late Michael Landon, told about Bryan who was only four years old when he was abducted by his father and his father's girlfriend. For four and one-half years Bryan lived in a trailer. He was not allowed to go to school; he never got to visit in anybody's home; he was seldom allowed outside the trailer.

Whenever his father felt it was no longer safe to stay where they were, he would move the trailer to a new location. Of course, Bryan's mother had reported his disappearance, and the police were searching for the child and his abductor.

One day Bryan's mother received a phone call from her ex-husband telling her that Bryan would be on a bus sometime that day. She and her new husband waited at the bus terminal for hours before the right bus pulled in. Bryan's stepfather was the first to recognize him after four years' absence. A child changes a great deal in four years. Bryan had never attended school, he had not been given adequate social contacts or opportunities to make friends with other children, and he had been generally neglected. The reason his father gave for abducting Bryan was that he didn't want to pay child support or have Bryan call his stepfather "Daddy number 2." [3]

A child who is forcibly removed from one of his parents, never to see him or her again, suffers immeasurably. Although the kidnapping parent may try to excuse the action by saying that he or she was concerned for the well-being of the child, the child is more often "used as a pawn by a parent to seek revenge for the breakup, to harass the estranged partner, to use as a 'bargaining chip' to reduce support obligations, or to extort a reconciliation. Often the abducting parent manipulates the child's loyalty—forcing the child to make an emotional choice between the two parents." [4] Being manipulated in any of these ways causes the child emotional trauma—anger, depression, guilt.

Added to the loss of one parent, the child also is separated from his home, school, pets, friends, and his extended family—grandparents, aunts, uncles, and cousins, creating even greater confusion, terror, and loneliness.

Janet Kosid-Uthe writes that "abducted children often experience inconsistent and erratic schooling, poverty, and isolation as the abducting parent moves frequently and changes employment to escape detection. When they are finally restored to their legal custodial parent, such children report experiencing anger, depression, guilt, and loneliness. These emotions are compounded if the abducting parent, under the stress of continued isolation and concealment, becomes abusive or neglectful."[5]

Sometimes, as happened with Bryan, the abducting parent will abandon the child when he gets tired of running or when he no longer wants the responsibility for care of the child.

Abandonment again severs the child from any family ties he may have begun to depend on. At least Bryan's father sent the boy home. Some children are abandoned in the apartment where they have been living or, worse, in a shopping mall, park, or other place.

How can this scenario be avoided? If you are a divorced parent and feel that there may be such an eventuality, how can you prepare your children? Obviously, you cannot say, "Don't let Daddy kidnap you this weekend." Someone must lay the groundwork long before divorce proceedings actually begin.

If you and your spouse are contemplating divorce, there are several things you can do to prepare your child for the ensuing changes.

- Maintain as much harmony as possible in your family relationships, even if you have to keep your disagreements between yourselves. Never argue in front of the children. Then, be civil to one another. No games, and no using the children. Children frequently believe that they have done something "bad" to cause their parents to split up. This is especially true if they have overheard their parents argue about them and their care.

- If possible, both parents should explain to the children that many things can damage a marriage, but that children are never the problem and never were.

- Contact your children's school and alert their teachers of the impending divorce. School authorities receive special training on helping children through divorce. See how you can work together with the school to smooth the way for your child.

- Inquire about professional counseling for your children during and after divorce. School counselors can be effective mediators in issues involving co-parenting, visitation rights, and possible abductions.

- Reassure your children that you don't expect them to take sides. They can continue to love both parents even after the divorce. Do not demean each other in the eyes of your children. Do not expect your children to choose sides, even if they are divided up between parents. Let them remain neutral and loyal to both parents.

- Encourage your children to talk about their feelings. Divorce is a family tragedy. Everyone is hurt. Help the children to talk about their fear, rejection, anger, or depression. Sometimes the family situation has been such that children feel relief when their parents are no longer living together. This should also be talked about so they feel no guilt for their relief.

- Unless your spouse has abandoned your family or is abusive or violent, children should know how to contact both parents in an emergency. They should know how to contact grandparents or aunts and uncles. Teach them how to use both rotary and push-button phones. Help them memorize phone numbers, including area codes. Tell them how to make a collect call or place a call through the operator, explaining when such calls should be made (or your phone bill may get out of hand).

- Have your children fingerprinted for possible future identification.

- Keep current photos of all the children.

- Have them practice writing letters, addressing the envelopes, and mailing them.

- Have them memorize the number for Child Find (1-800-A-WAY-OUT), which helps parents locate their lost children.

- Assure your children that you will never abandon them. Tell them that if they should lose contact with you or wonder why they have not seen you, they should call you or some other member of the family or the Child Find number.

Non-Family Abduction

On the CBS special, "America's Missing Children," Patty and Jerry Wetterling told about their son Jacob's abduction. It took place in a small town in northern Minnesota, not on the streets of New York or Los Angeles. Jacob, his brother, and a friend rode their bicycles to the video store just at dark. They wore light-colored clothing, reflector vests, and carried flashlights. Jerry said he felt that his fifth- and sixth-grade sons would be safe riding the short distance to the store.

On the way back from the store the boys were stopped by a man wearing a mask and carrying a gun. He made the boys lie down on the ground. He grabbed Jacob and ran off with him into the night. The other two boys rode home as fast as they could and told their parents what had happened. Within hours a massive manhunt was underway. Over the next few weeks authorities received *fifty thousand* leads, none of which turned up a viable suspect. Jacob has not yet been found. His parents established a Jacob Wetterling Foundation. And flyers and other notices about Jacob's disappearance are still being sent all over the country by volunteers.

A U.S. Department of Justice publication stated that an estimated 3,200 to 4,600 non-family abductions occurred in 1988. These were "coerced and unauthorized *taking* of a child into a building, a vehicle, or a distance of more than twenty feet; the *detention* of a child for a period of more than an hour; or the *luring* of a child for the purposes of committing another crime, such as sexual assault."[6] An estimated 200-300 of these were committed by a stranger.

Federal Bureau of Investigation data indicate that many kidnapped children are eventually killed. The national incidence study showed that children are abducted by strangers for sexual exploitation, ritualistic abuse, black market sale of infants, profit, or ransom. Half of the victims were age twelve or older; three-quarters were females; minorities were more likely to be abducted by strangers or non-family members who may be known by the parents or the children.[7]

In the CBS special, James Kirk told about his attempted abduction when he was only six years old. He went to the movies with his mother. He wanted to go to the restroom, and his mother felt he could go by himself. Seated near the exit was Westley Allen Dodd, a man who had a fourteen-year history of molesting children and who had murdered two brothers, ages four and nine. When James walked up the aisle and passed Dodd, the kidnapper got up and followed the boy into the restroom. When James started back to the theater, Dodd picked him up and told him to be quiet. As Dodd carried James through the theater lobby, the boy kicked, struggled, and screamed, "This isn't my dad." Dodd said, "Calm down, son." Theater employees were suspicious and while one person called the police, others followed the man outside as he struggled with the screaming, kicking youngster. When the abductor got to the parking lot he put James down and ran off.

After he was apprehended and arrested Dodd stated that he spent his time around movie theaters, parks, playgrounds—wherever children would be—looking for his victims. He said that he gave up if the child he snatched attracted the attention of people in the area. James had been properly trained in how to deal with such an incident.

This training is especially critical for little girls. While young boys will likely fight an abductor in a "macho" way, young girls will not. Three-quarters of child abduction victims are female, with minorities even more vulnerable. Parents should teach and practice methods for self-protection so that children will react without fear or helplessness:

- See to it that your small children are always supervised when they are playing. Warn them not to play near wooded areas. Be sure they stay near other people when they play at playgrounds or parks.

- Accompany them when they go to any public restroom. At least follow them there and wait until they come out.

- Have your child practice how she would scream, "You're hurting me. You're not my daddy (mommy)! Let me go!" if someone grabs her. Some children are reticent to attract attention. Assure them that sometimes it is all right—even necessary—to make an enormous scene.

- Tell your children that it is not okay for anyone to touch them in the "bathing suit" areas of their bodies. The three guidelines are *No, Go,* and *Tell.* If they are touched in private places—or anywhere on their bodies—they have the right to say, *No,* the right to *Go* or get away from the scene, and the right to *Tell* someone about the incident.

- Be sure your children know how to use the telephone, that they have memorized their own numbers as well as those of extended family members, and that they know how to call 911.

- When your latchkey child is home alone, be sure that he keeps the doors locked and that he does not answer the door at all, for any reason, when an adult is not home.

- Warn them about accepting rides with any non-family member unless you specify which ones are acceptable.

- Encourage them to tell you or a teacher any "secret" an adult tries to make them keep. Assure the child that you will not allow him or yourself to be hurt or killed if he betrays this secret.

- When you are out with your child, be aware of potentially dangerous situations that you can bring to your child's attention—such as a stranger sitting alone on a park bench, or a stranger talking to children playing on a playground.

- Teach them not to take candy or money or toys or anything from a stranger.

- Role-playing stories such as "Little Red Riding Hood" is a good way to teach children about dangerous strangers.

- Play "what-if" and present different situations your child may find himself in and what he would do to get out of them.

- Encourage the "buddy system." Teach your child to walk home from school with other children and not to go anywhere alone.

- Encourage your child to follow rules of responsible behavior and to ignore peer pressure.

- Even young children can learn self- defense methods such as biting, screaming, kicking, and scratching. Classes in karate or other self- defense programs are helpful, too. (Contact The Children's Safety Series, Charles Franklin Press, 7821 175th St. S.W., Edmonds, WA 98020, phone 206-774-6979.)

Kidnapping is a problem that deserves attention. However, these incidents are few in comparison to the millions of children who are never kidnapped. Parents should be cautious, but not to the extent that they instill fear in their children or disrupt their lives over something that very well could never happen. But, since kidnapping is just one more danger your child should be aware of, it is your responsibility to prepare him for such an eventuality.

What Works

1. Teach us what to do if we are grabbed. Practice with us. Teach us the difference between being fearful of people and being wisely cautious of them.

13

Street Violence

L os Angeles County has earned the reputation of being one of the most dangerous places in the world. In 1991, more than eight thousand people—almost one an hour—were hit by aimed or random bullets. (This is thirteen times more gunshot victims than there were U.S. military killed and wounded during the Persian Gulf war.) More Los Angeles people died from gunshot wounds than from traffic accidents. Added to these statistics are those who were stabbed, bludgeoned, or strangled. Most of these incidents were in areas where gang warfare is common, but many times they were drive-by or freeway shootings and muggings. And more than a quarter of these victims were nineteen years old or younger![1]

These alarming and depressing facts take on even greater grimness when the victims are innocent children. On an average day, six American children will be slain.[2] In one tenth-grade class at a Laurel, Maryland, high school with an enrollment of twenty-six students, sixteen of them knew of a person under nineteen years old who had been killed. Thirteen knew of someone who had been stabbed.[3] In 1988, homicide ranked fourth as the cause of death for children under age fourteen, and homicide was the leading cause of death by injury for those under one year.[4]

Ask your children to tell you if they ever feel afraid when they are walking alone on your town's streets, and you will discover that they feel fear even if they have never experienced or witnessed acts of violence.

Many city dwellers avoid getting on elevators, going to parks, malls, the beach, or any public gathering, and even hesitate to use automatic bank machines in broad daylight for fear of getting caught in crossfire, being mugged or raped. Residents imprison themselves behind barred windows and triple-locked doors as soon as the sun goes down and do not emerge until daylight, and even then they watch behind them, cringe when a car they do not recognize comes down the street, or cross the road if they see a group of people standing on the sidewalk.

A *Los Angeles Times* poll revealed that street violence has changed the way people live in the city. Thirty-one percent of those responding to the poll said they are more cautious; 18 percent have installed a home security system; 11 percent will not let their children play outside; 11 percent no longer go out alone; 10 percent do not take walks as they used to; 6 percent say they have moved or are planning to.[5]

Not every family can move out of the city where they live and work. They should not be expected to. But they can take steps to bring safety back to their streets. Parents need to cooperate with city, county, and federal authorities that are trying to rid their streets of drugs, gangs, and other criminal influences that cause violence. However, until we take charge of our cities and towns once again, we must take charge of our children and teach them how to protect themselves where violence is rampant.

Even if you live in towns that are fairly safe, your children should know how to avoid potentially dangerous situations. For example, children should be aware that elevators are not always safe places to be. If your child or teenager is alone, she should not enter an elevator if only one other person is inside. She should wait for the next elevator. If she is the only one who boards on the ground floor and the elevator stops on the second floor to let on a lone man, she should get off at the next floor. She should always stand near the alarm button just in case. If she is attacked she should scream as loud as she can and push the alarm button.

Children should take the same precautions in other parts of the city where they could be in danger. These include parks, malls, shopping centers, movie theaters, school grounds, alleys, bus stops, in the halls, parking and storage areas of apartment buildings, and of course, cars when hitchhiking or picking up hitchhikers. These are the places where murder, mugging, and rape can occur.

There is little we can do to protect ourselves from a sniper's bullet or a drive-by shooting, but we can do much to avoid other dangers. One of the most common horrors our children will encounter is that of sexual assault. We read much about children being molested in their own homes by someone they know. But there are probably more incidents of children being assaulted outside of the safety of their homes; they just do not report the incident because of embarrassment, guilt, or fear.

Sexual Assault

According to "Rape and Assault," published by The Coalition Against Household Violence of Ventura County, the category of sexual assault can include rape, incest, sexual harassment, child molestation, marital rape, exposure, and voyeurism. Definitions vary among states. Since many misconceptions exist about sexual assault, we should know and make sure our children know the *facts:*

- Victims of sexual assault do not cause their assaults. Offenders are responsible for the assaults.

- Sexual assaults are committed primarily out of anger and/or a need to feel powerful, to control and dominate another person.

- Victims of sexual assaults are forced, coerced, or manipulated to participate in sexual activity.

- Victims are traumatized by the assault. Friends or family members may also experience trauma.

- Sexual assaults are crimes. They can be reported to the police and the offenders prosecuted in court.[6]

Sexual assault creates barriers between family members, co-workers, students, and friends, regardless of who it happens to. It is a major life crisis. A person who has been sexually assaulted suffers several emotional and physical consequences: sleeplessness, lack of concentration, overeating or appetite loss, nightmares, loss of self-confidence, stress-related illness, feelings of grief and despair. The victim may have fears of night or dark, of being alone or of being around other people, of various settings and people, and so on. Recovery can be slow, but it will go better if trained counselors who understand the needs of sexual assault victims are brought into the process. Most large communities have rape crisis centers and twenty-four-hour hotlines and a specially trained counseling staff.[7]

Sexual assault is not limited to girls and women. In fact, boys and men are frequently assaulted by other men. Rape can happen to anyone—children, grandmothers, students, working men and women, mothers, wives, the rich, and the poor. It can occur just about anyplace where the rapist may not be easily interrupted. About two-thirds of all rapes occur in or near the victim's own home,[8] and often the victim knows the rapist.

Date Rape

Children are becoming sexually active at a much earlier age than they used to. Encouraged by movies and TV, they begin to experiment with sex in elementary school. Girls sixteen to nineteen years old, the most sexually victimized, are getting raped in numbers never seen before.

Forcible rape occurs every six minutes in the U.S.[9] One in three girls and women will be raped either by a date or a stranger sometime in her lifetime.[10] Girls will almost never report a date rape to their parents, and only one in ten women will report rape attacks to the police.[11]

Far too often, when law officers receive a report, they investigate the allegation. Of those incidents investigated, only a portion reach the district attorney's office. The D.A.'s office will prosecute none but the strongest cases, those he or she is sure to win. The prosecuting attorneys, wanting to avoid the hassles and uncertainties of a protracted trial on an already overloaded court calendar, will convince the defendant to plea bargain to a lesser crime. By now the girl really feels victimized and the rapist goes virtually free.

The Scroll, published by Phi Delta Theta fraternity, ran an article by Jim Hoppe, a faculty advisor. He stated that one in six college women will be the victim of a sexual assault or rape and that 90 percent of gang rapes are linked by the media to fraternities. He believes that these attacks occur because of alcohol or drug abuse, miscommunication, and an overreliance on stereotypes. Ninety percent of all campus rapes involve the use of drugs or alcohol, which reduces the man's willingness to communicate and listen to the woman, and heightens his reliance on societal stereotype that men who "score" pass their test of manhood. According to this credo, if a woman says no, a real man will not take no for an answer; therefore, he forces himself on her to prove his manhood.[12]

But date rape and violence often occur before a girl reaches college. Fifteen-year-old Jenny Crompton was a victim of dating violence in a semi-rural area of Iowa. She had not been going with Mark Smith very long before he began to slap her and shove her around. Jenny tried many times to break off the tumultuous relationship, but he refused to let her go and she was afraid of him.

On September 26, 1986, Smith stabbed Jenny sixty times with a butcher knife. He is now serving a sentence for murder. Jenny's family did not know that Jenny and Mark's relationship had been abusive until they read about it in the paper on the day of Jenny's funeral. Police interviews with Jenny's friends revealed that from the very beginning of their relationship Mark had abused Jenny, threatened her verbally and in notes, and spied on her.

Jenny's mother, Vicki Crompton, now spends time speaking to adolescents about dating violence. She says that she can always tell which teenagers are in abusive relationships by watching their eyes. Mrs. Crompton gives the following advice to parents whose daughters are in romantic relationships. Ask:

- Is the boyfriend possessive or does he try to isolate the girl? When Jenny refused to give up her friends when Mark wanted her to, he made her friends his friends and used them to further his possession of Jenny.

- Does he talk about their future? Jenny laughed about Mark talking about their wedding. She had no plans for a wedding; she wanted to go to college and live in Europe.

- Do you know the boyfriend and his family? Mark would never talk to Jenny's parents about his home or himself. Vickie heard in court how Mark had emotional problems from the time he was four years old, how his mother moved out of their home when Mark was only sixteen because he was so violent.

Parents should teach their daughters how to break up firmly and finally. This is no time for a girl to "feel sorry" for a person. Jenny did have the courage to tell Mark that she just wanted to be friends, but she could not tell him never to call her or come around again. It was a fatal error.[13]

Laura knew all Billy's friends, they had grown up together for years, they had played touch football and one-on-one basketball together after school. They were pals. She was as comfortable with them as she was with her own brother.

No one else was home when one of Billy's friends began to get a little bit rowdier with Laura. Before Laura knew what was happening, he had her pinned down and was forcibly grabbing at body parts he had never touched before, and he had a different look in his eyes. Laura went into stun mode, and before she knew it, it was over.

Her "pal" had raped her.

She cried in uncontrollable sobs as she showered for two hours with the hottest water she could tolerate to remove all traces of the attack.

She felt far too dirty, too ashamed, and too afraid to tell anyone what had happened, so she just lived with the hideously ugly memory burned deeply into her mind.[14]

Even though the decision to have forcible sex, in short, to rape, is a conscious one, date rapists generally don't see their act of forced sex as the same as a predatory opportunist rapist lying in wait or on the prowl. Some date rapists do, and clearly know for many reasons that the justice system is simply not able to move toward securing a conviction.

Some date rapists operate on the highly mistaken and rather caveman-like view that all women like—no, actually desire—sexual coercion, and that the act of sex has to contain an element of force to release the animal heat of sex for the woman.

Parallel to such tragic logic is the man's mistaken notion that nice girls need some excuse to explain—if to no one else then certainly to themselves—why sex happened. If a girl can say it was forced, she needn't take personal responsibility for anything that happened.

Teach Your Children About Sexual Assault

For many of us, talking with our children about sex is not easy. We are concerned that we will say too much or too little, will begin too soon or too late. We worry about the words we use and about whether we can effectively communicate in a relaxed manner or disclose some of our own hang-ups on the issue. As if this were not enough, we are not being told that we must go beyond discussing sex and must begin talking to our children not only about sex but sexual abuse and ways of protecting themselves from it. This issue poses many questions: How do we do this? When should we do this? What should we say?

Present the information in an open, honest, and factual manner. Don't scare your kids, but let them know that children are being abused. The best tool you have is communication: Talk to your children. Let them know you are deeply concerned about their safety and that you are somebody with whom they can discuss these issues.

Start by offering them a working knowledge of all the body parts. This helps you talk about sexual assault in the specific terms necessary to provide useful information.

Talk about different kinds of touch. Explain that good touch is a hug, a handshake, a pat on the back; bad touch is a push, a punch, a kick. *Secret* touch involves the touching of private parts (stick to the terms you have already established for the genitals). Secret touch can involve another person touching a child's private parts or forcing a child to touch his or her private parts. Explain that this type of touch often involves some degree of nudity as well. This kind of touch is very confusing because the perpetrator may be someone the child knows, likes, or even loves. Secret touch is not the child's secret but the secret of the offender.

Avoid describing child sexual assault as "bad" touch. It is bad from our perspective, but since sexual touch generally feels good, the child may like the touch, especially in the beginning stages of ongoing assault. Also, the child may receive favors, gifts, and special attention from the abuser. These always seem good. Further, if the child likes or even loves the offender, he or she will not want to hear the term "bad" associated with this person who is doing such nice things. Often when children hear the word "bad" they tend to think that they are being blamed for the incident. It is best to explain that secret touch is a *confusing* touch, not a bad touch, that what the offender did was wrong, and that the child is not to blame for the abuser's actions.

Explain the difference between sexual assault and sex. Tell children that sexual assault is something that happens to them without their permission. For example, when they close their bedroom doors they are saying "No Trespassing" without permission. They have a right to say "No Trespassing" on their bodies also.

To avoid confusion, explain that there are times when people are asked to take off their clothes and allow their genitals to be touched, such as when going to a doctor. Since this is not secret or confusing touch, it is not sexual assault.

Tell your children that they have the right to make decisions about their own bodies. For example, "Your body belongs to you. You can decide who touches it. If somebody wants to pat your bottom, you can tell them not to. If somebody touches your breasts, you can say, 'Don't do that to me.'"

Assure them of your support in not wanting to be touched. Then be sure to protect them from unwanted touch, such as when a stranger tries to hug or kiss them, or even when a relative grabs and tries to kiss them. Enthusiastic relatives love to hug and kiss children. But forcing children to submit to this kind of attention gives wrong signals. Children should be allowed to give their affection freely, without force from parents or others, and they will if the conditions are right.

In the event of sexual assault, support and praise the child for telling you. Do not overreact! Most young kids do not understand the impact of sexual assault and may not be traumatized by the incident. But if you make a big deal out of it by becoming upset and overreacting in an extreme, dramatic manner, you may compound the incident in the child's mind.

Continue to warn them about strangers. Even though most children are assaulted by someone they know, you should tell your children not to accept any gifts, invitations, or rides from strangers.

Tell them that they should look straight ahead when they are walking down the street. They should ignore attention and attempts to get their attention. Whenever possible, they should walk with friends, not alone.

Make up a code word for your child. In the event that someone other than you picks up your child from school or other activity, have him or her be sure to ask what the code word is. They should not accept the ride, even if they know the person, if the driver does not know the code.

Teach your children to respect their intuition and gut feeling. If they do not feel good about a situation, it is important to listen to those feelings and try to get out of the situation immediately.

Children can be taught safety issues as soon as they begin to talk. If you feel uncomfortable about this subject, rehearse until you feel more at ease. Remember that your kids will sense any discomfort you feel. Try not to explain everything at once, but perhaps begin with a discussion about body parts and then gradually bring up sexual assault and safety. Furthermore, parents should not assume that once discussed, the topic can be closed. These issues should be discussed frequently.[15]

Reduce Their Risks

Because many sexual assaults happen on the street or at a park, playground, or school yard, your children should know what they can do to protect themselves. Teenagers often have to walk home after dark from an after-school job, a friend's home, football practice, or other school activity. Teach them the safety measures they should always observe:

- Stay in well-lit areas as much as possible.

- Walk confidently and at a steady pace. A rapist looks for someone who appears vulnerable.

- Walk on the side of the street nearest traffic.

- Walk close to the curb. Avoid doorways, bushes, and alleys where a rapist can hide.

- If you think you are being followed, walk quickly to areas where there are lights and people. If a car appears to be following you, turn quickly, cross the street, and walk in the opposite direction.

- Be careful when people in cars ask you for directions. Always reply from a distance and never get close to the car.

- If you believe you are in danger, don't be reluctant to scream and run. Consider carrying a whistle or any type of noisemaker. And, if you're in trouble, use it!

- If you are in trouble, attract help in any way you can. Scream, yell for help, yell "Fire!" or break the nearest window. Remember that if a weapon is involved, your choices will be limited.[16]

What Works

1. Teach us how to "walk tall": Look a person in the eye before passing him, and look unafraid as if saying, "I know you're here, but I don't care."

2. Teach us how to have our eyes and ears open all the time, even while walking and talking with a friend. Show us how you stay aware when you're out on your own.

PART IV

One
Last
Word

One Last Word

As a final wrap-up to this project, we offer the following two lists that will afford your children the kind of atmosphere they need to develop to their fullest. Keeping in mind that kids orient themselves to things that are sources of nourishment and nurturing, and since they automatically pursue things that feed them physically, emotionally, and spiritually, every parent would do well to make sure the following guidelines are put into practice, creating the kind of home atmosphere that kids love to experience. The first list is those qualities which give your kids the best chance for entering adulthood in the healthiest and safest way possible. The second list is a kid's bill of rights that, if put into practice, will guarantee that your child will become the kind of adult who will make you very proud.

What to Do About Leveling the Field and Setting Up Boundaries:

Treat them with respect.

Set a good example.

Challenge them with achievable goals.

Compliment them. Catch them doing something right.

Get and stay active in your kids' world. Be a positive enabler for your kids.

Give them responsibility in reasonable doses.

Keep communication lines open.

Children won't wait—be available, be there.

When your kids reach the age of thirteen, shift parenting style from boss to wise man.

Keep commitments you make to your children.

Go ahead and lay down house rules, but back them up with logical explanations and your own example.

Remember that the job of parenting is to be a lifeguard in shark-infested waters. Stay on duty. Never fall asleep for a moment.

Punish from a cool head and a warm heart.

Get to know your kids' friends.

Get to know your kids' friends' parents.

Get to know your kids anew once in a while. They do change over time.

It's okay to be your kids' friend, but remember you're a parent first and foremost. It's okay to pull rank to lay down or back up rules.

When push comes to shove, your kids do have to obey you. See that they do.

Rules should deal with your kids' safety. Be sure they do, and be sure you can explain their logic.

Remember that parenting is inherently inconveniencing. Don't look for it to be very easy. Make sure your rules speak to what's best for your kids, not what makes life easiest for you. In other words, while reinforcing the rule that your kid not be lazy, don't be lazy regarding your parenting (or your own life).

Admit mistakes: not theirs, yours!

Be warm, loving, considerate, approachable, polite. Being these things doesn't mean you're a softy or a pushover. If you want your kids to respect you, respect them.

Hug your kids a lot.

Make your home an open and welcome place to be, a place that attracts your children and their friends.

Find out what they're interested in and then become the supplier/provider of that. Don't decide yourself what they should be interested in and shove them toward that. They'll resist, as would you if someone else did that to you.

Teach them discipline and responsibility by helping them find and get into activities that they love, which demand discipline and responsibility in themselves. Then sit back and watch discipline and responsibility spring into existence as a result of those activities.

Let them see you as their biggest fan by being their biggest fan.

Praise them and send them praise notes/cards often.

Say that you're proud of them.

Be willing to lay down your own activity to listen to your kids when they come in excited to tell you about something neat in their world.

Remember that your kids are not in this world to cater to you or jump to your expectations or demands. They have their own agendas, and you must respect them.

Go out of your busy way to do nice things for your kids.

Don't deplete yourself completely emotionally during your workday. Keep some niceness and patience in reserve for when you get home and are hit at the front door with a wave of parenting chores and kid-requests.

When your kids have to be alone by necessity of your work schedule—call them often—hourly or so, so that they sense your closeness and concern.

Parenting can be exhausting work with little payback for a long time. Don't expect it to be otherwise. You'll just frustrate yourself and your kid.

Provide spiritual anchoring.

Learn to laugh at them and at yourself.

Stay in touch: the top banana keeps in touch with the bunch.

What Kids Need to Come of Age
Safety-Smart Kids Have an Inalienable Right to:

A home that is viewed by them clearly as a place of safe haven where they can recharge their batteries or lick their daily wounds; where their parents sympathize, but don't baby.

A home where warm affection is openly and freely expressed, as are altruistic love, encouragement, support, positive recognition, respect, reasonable expectations, approval, trust, all in abundant amounts.

A home where parents are actively involved—but not overly so—in engaging hobbies, and who—without indulging them materialistically—make fun things available to their kids above and beyond what the kids can provide for themselves.

A home where carefully arranged and thoughtfully articulated structure and reasonable limits and expectations clearly show the kids what and where their (valued) place is.

A home where Mom and Dad clearly and openly love, respect, and care deeply for each other.

A home of regular family outings that show the kids how to constructively have some fun.

A home where the parents gradually and steadily relax their control over their kids as their kids demonstrate their ability to limit and control themselves. Part of the relaxing of control involves a parental shift from direct hands-on kid-control of prepubertal and pubertal kids to more consultative influence as kids move beyond puberty into mid and late teen years.

A home where intra-sibling conflict is handled with humor and fun.
A home where anger is allowed constructive outlet.

A home where both parents consistently model the values they teach; they painstakingly practice the values they preach.

A home where parents teach responsibility and discipline by their own practice of it and by helping their kids engage in exciting superhobbies that demand responsibility and discipline.

A home where tenderness to and consideration for others is regularly practiced.

A home where parents show willingness—without complaint—to defer their own needs for the sake of the needs of their kids.

A home where too heavy a load of responsibility isn't relegated onto kids too early for them to handle it.

A home where a "higher moral road to travel, and higher moral ground to stand on is taught by way of" morals taught and morals caught by parental teaching and by unwavering and conscientious parental practice and example.

A home where the development of a higher moral self is encouraged and supported by parental example and instruction.

A home where tolerance for all people is taught by instruction and example.

Where to Go for Help

Chapter 2 Latchkey Child

Books

Bergstrom, Joan M. *School's Out—Now What? Creative Choices for Your Child.* Berkeley, CA: Ten Speed Press, rev. ed. 1990.

Buchanan, Cynthia Dee; Thomas J. Paul; and Peg Long, *Safe At Home, Safe Alone.* Miles River Press, 1985. (Order from Kidrights, 3700 Progress Blvd., Mount Dora, FL 32757; 800-892-5437.)

Chaback, Elaine, and Pat Fortunato, *The Official Kids' Survival Kit: How to Do Things on Your Own.* Boston, MA: Little, Brown & Co., 1981.

Kyte, Kathy. *Play It Safe: The Kids, Guide to Personal Safety & Crime Prevention.* New York: Alfred A. Knopf, 1983.

Long, Lynette. *On My Own: The Kids' Self Care Book.* Washington, D.C.: Acropolis Books, Ltd., 1984.

Paul, Aileen. *Kids Cooking Without a Stove: A Cookbook for Young Children.* Garden City, NY: Doubleday & Co., Inc., 1975.

Phillips, Phil. *52 Things for Your Kids to Do Instead of Watching TV.* Nashville, TN: Thomas Nelson Publishers, 1992.

Stanek, Muriel. *All Alone After School.* Morton Grove, IL: Albert Whitman & Company, 1985.

Organizations

Big Brothers/Big Sisters of America
230 N. 13th St.
Philadelphia, PA 19107
215-567-7000

Boy Scouts of America, Inc.
1325 Walnut Hill Lane
Irving, TX 75015-2079
214-580-2000

Girl Scouts of the U.S.A.
830 Third Avenue
New York, NY 10022
212-940-7500

Boys Clubs of America
771 First Avenue
New York, NY 10017
212-351-5900

Girls Clubs of America
30 E. 33rd St.
New York, NY 10016
212-689-3700

CampFire, Inc.
4601 Madison Avenue
Kansas City, MO 64112
816-756-1950

Parents Without Partners
8807 Colesville Rd.
Silver Springs, MD 20910
301-588-9354

YMCA of the United States
101 North Wacker Drive
Chicago, IL 60606
312-977-0031

YWCA of the United States of America
726 Broadway
New York, NY 10003
212-614-2700

Chapter 3 Firearms

Books

My Gun Safety Book
National Rifle Association of America
Educational & Training Division
1600 Rhode Island Avenue, N.W.
Washington, D.C. 20036
202-828-6000

Organizations

Educational Fund to End Handgun Violence
Box 72
110 Maryland Avenue, N.E.
Washington, D.C. 20002
202-544-7227

Handgun Control, Inc.
1225 Eye Street, N.W., Suite 1100
Washington, D.C. 20005
202-898-0792

National Coalition to Ban Handguns
100 Maryland Avenue, N.E.
Washington, D.C. 20002-5625
202-544-7190

National Rifle Association
1600 Rhode Island Avenue, N.W.
Washington, D.C. 20036
202-828-6000

Chapter 4 Alcohol

Books

Dobson, James C. *Parenting Isn't for Cowards.* Colorado Springs, CO: Focus on the Family Publishers.

Englebrandt, Stanley L. *Kids & Alcohol, The Deadliest Drug.* New York: Lothrop, 1975.

Gold, Mark S. *The Facts About Drugs & Alcohol.* New York: Bantam Books, 1988.

Howard, Marion. *Did I Have a Good Time? Teenage Drinking.* New York: Continuum Pub. Co., 1982.

Huggins, Kevin. *Parenting Adolescents.* Colorado Springs, CO: NavPress, 1989.

Organizations

Alateen, Al-Anon Family Group Headquarters, Inc.
Box 862 Midtown Station
New York, NY 10018
212-302-7240

Mothers Against Drunk Driving (MADD)
National Office
511 E. John Carpenter Fwy. #700
Irving, TX 75062
214-744-6233

National Teen Challenge
1525 N. Campbell Ave.
Springfield, MO 65803
417-862-6969

STRAIGHT, for teens
3001 Gandy Boulevard
St. Petersburg, FL 33702
881-576-8929

Chapter 5 Bullies

Books

Carlson, Nancy. *Loudmouth George and the Sixth-Grade Bully.* New York: Puffin Books, 1987.

de Paola, Tomie. *Andy (That's My Name).* New York: Prentice Hall, 1972. (Ages 3-5).

Garcia, Maria. *The Adventures of Connie and Diego/Los Aventuras De Connie Y Diego.* Emeryville, CA: Children's Book Press, 1987. (Ages 4-8).

Rogers, Mister (Fred). *Making Friends.* New York: Putnam, 1987. (Preschool).

Stolz, Mary. *The Bully of Barkham Street.* New York: Harper & Row, 1989. (Junior High, One of three in a boxed set.)

Waber, Bernard. *You Look Ridiculous, Said the Rhinoceros to the Hippopotamus.* Boston: Houghton Mifflin, 1970. (Ages 5-8).

Audio-Visual

The following could be purchased by your school, church group, or youth organization

Nobody Likes a Bully, narrated by Bill Cosby (film 15 minutes). School of Education, Winthrop College, Rock Hill, SC 29733. 803-323-2151. Cost: $100.

Set Straight on Bullies, (Film and videotape, 18 minutes). National School Safety Center, 16830 Ventura Blvd., Suite 200, Encino, CA 91436. Cost: VHS and Beta, $40; 16mm film, $200.

Chapter 6 Gangs

Books

Campbell, Joseph. *The Power of Myth.* New York: Doubleday Books, 1988.

Gangs in School: Breaking Up Is Hard to Do. Malibu, CA: National School Safety Center, Pepperdine University, 1993.

Jackson, Robert K., and Wesley D. McBride. *Street Gangs, Understanding.* Placerville, CA: Copperhouse Pub. Co., 1989.

Kahaner, Larry. *Cults That Kill: Probing the Underworld of Occult Crime.* New York: Warner Books, 1989.

Larson, Bob. *Satanism: The Seduction of America's Youth.* Nashville, TN: Thomas Nelson Publishers, 1989.

Chapter 7 Drugs

Books

The following booklets, published by the U.S. Department of Health, Education, and Welfare, Public Health Service, and Alcohol, Drug Abuse and Mental Health Administration, are for sale by the Superintendent of Documents, U.S. Government Printing Office, Washington, D.C. 20402.

Drug Abuse Prevention for Your Family

Drug Abuse Prevention for You and Your Friends

Drug Abuse Prevention for Your Community

Drug Abuse Prevention (general audience)

La Prevencion del Abuso de Drogas (Spanish)

Ellis, Dan C., *Growing Up Stoned.* Deerfield Beach, FL: Health Communications, 1986.

Mann, Peggy. *The Sad Story of Mary Wanna or How Marijuana Harms You.* New York: Woodmere Press, 1988. Elementary level reading material. P. O. Box 20190, Park West Finance Station, New York, NY 10025.

Robertson, Dr. Joel C. *Kids Don't Want to Use Drugs* (or drink, or overeat, or smoke. How you and your kids can avoid the dangers.) Nashville, TN: Thomas Nelson Publishers, 1992.

Tobias, Joyce M. *Kids and Drugs: A Handbook for Parents and Professionals.* Annandale, VA: Panda Press, 1989.

Organizations

Alcohol and Drug Abuse Education Program (ADAEP)
U.S. Department of Education
400 Maryland, S.W.
Washington, D.C. 20202-6151
202-732-4599

Narcotics Anonymous
World Service Office
P. O. Box 9999
Van Nuys, CA 91409
818-780-3951

National Institute of Drug Abuse Hotline
800-662-HELP

Teen Challenge
Training Center
P. O. Box 198
Rehrersburg, PA 19550
717-933-4181

Toughlove
P. O. Box 1069
Doylestown, PA 18901
215-348-7090

Chapter 8 Sexual Involvement

Books

Gordon, Sol, and Judith Gordon. *A Family Guide for Sexual Assault Prevention, A Better Safe Than Sorry Book.* Fayettfille, NY: Ed-U Press, Inc., 1984.

Ozer, Elizabeth M. & Nkenge, Toure. *Staying Safe: How to Protect Yourself Against Sexual Assault.* Washington, D.C.: Rape Crisis Center, 1984.

Parrot, Andrea. *Coping with Date Rape & Acquaintance Rape.* New York: Rosen Pub. Group, 1988.

Quackenbush, Marci, ed. *The AIDS Challenge—Prevention Education for Young People.* Santa Cruz, CA: ETR Assoc., 1988.

Sandvig, Karen. *Falling into the Big L.* Ventura, CA: Regal Books, 1989.

——. *You're What? Help & Hope for Pregnant Teens.* Ventura, CA: Regal Books, 1988.

Stephens, Andrea. *Stressed Out ... But Hangin Tough!* Old Tappan, NJ: Fleming H. Revell Company, 1989.

What Young Adults Should Know (about AIDS). Waldorf, MD: AAHPERD, P O Box 704, Waldorf, MD 20604, 1987.

Chapter 11   Your Part in Making Schools Safer

Books

Preventing Violence: Program Ideas and Examples. Published by the
National Crime Prevention Council
1700 K Street NW, Second Floor
Washington, D.C. 20006-3817
202-466-6272

School Violence: A Survival Guide for School Staff
NEA Professional Library
P.O. Box 509
West Haven, CT 06516
800-229-4200

Organizations

National Alliance for Safe Schools
6931 Arlington Rd. Suite 400
Bethesda, MD 20814
301-907-7888

National School Safety Center
Pepperdine University
Malibu, CA 90263

National Child Safety Council
P.O. Box 1368
Jackson, MI 49204

SAFE POLICY
Office of Juvenile Justice and Delinquency Prevention
U.S. Department of Justice
633 Indiana Avenue, NW
Washington, D.C. 20531

Student Crime Stoppers International, Inc., offers a program for reporting campus crime. Contact them at:
Student Crime Stoppers International, Inc.
3736 Eubank Blvd. NE Suite B-4
Albuquerque, NM 87111
505-294-2300

The Education Development Center has produced "Violence Prevention: A Curriculum" by Deborah Prothrow-Stith, which examines the importance of preventing violence and providing alternatives to such behavior. Write or call:
Education Development Center
55 Chapel St. Suite 24
Newton, MA 02160
800-225-4276

STAR (Straight Talk About Risks) is a pre-kindergarten through grade 12 curriculum that teaches students about decision-making, conflict management, and other skills necessary for them to react properly if they encounter a gun. Contact:
The Center to Prevent Handgun Violence
1225 Eye Street NW Suite 1100
Washington, D.C. 20005
202-289-7319

Chapter 12 Abduction

Books

The following titles are in The Children's Safety Series and can be ordered from Charles Franklin Press, Edmonds, WA.

Private Zone

Safety Zone

It's Not Your Fault

Dial "0" for Help

Help Yourself to Safety, I Take Good Care of Me (coloring book)

Strangers Don't Look Like the Big Bad Wolf

The Kid-Ability. Omaha, NE: Girls Club of Omaha, 3706 Lake Street, Omaha, NE 68111.

Meyer, Linda D. *Safety Zone: A Book Teaching Children Abduction Prevention Skills.* Edmonds, WA: Franklin Press, 1984.

Strickland, Margaret. *How to Deal with a Parental Kidnapping.* Moore Haven, FL: Rainbow Books, 1984.

Organizations

Child Find
P. O. Box 277
New Paltz, NY 12561
914-255-1848
800-A-WAY-OUT

National Center for Missing and Exploited Children
2101 Wilson Blvd., Suite 550
Arlington, VA 22201
703-235-3900
800-843-5678

Chapter 13   Street Violence

Books

Buscaglia, Leo. *The Fall of Freddie the Leaf.* Thorofare, NJ: Slack, Inc., 1982.

Girard, Linda Walvoord. *Who Is a Stranger and What Should I Do?* Morton Grove, IL: Albert Whitman and Co., 1985.

Order the following from King County Rape Relief, P. O. Box 300, Renton, WA 98057.

Be Aware. Be Safe. 1987.

El Me Dijo Que No Se Lo Contara A Nadie. 1979

Fay, Jennifer J. *He Told Me Not to Tell.* 1979

Writtet, Scott, and Debbie Wong. *Helping Your Child to Be Safe.* KCSA Res. Center, 1987.

Stringer, Gayle M., and Deanna Ranchs-Rodriguez. *So What's It to Me? Sexual Assault Information for Guys. 1987.*

Model Programs & Resources

Center for the Study of Parent Involvement
5237 College Avenue
Oakland, California 96418

Cities in Schools
1023 15th Street, NW
Suite 600
Washington, D. C. 20005
202-861-0230

Drug and Alcohol Help Line
4578 Highland Drive
Salt Lake City, UT 84117
800-821-4357

Family and School Connections Project
Center for Research of Elementary and Middle Schools
John Hopkins University
3505 North Charles Street
Baltimore, MD 21218
301-726-4750

Family Resource Coalition
230 North Michigan
Suite 1625
Chicago, IL 60601
312-726-4750

Helping Youth Decide
National Association of State Boards of Education
Post Office Box 1176
Alexandria, VA 22313
703-684-4000

Institute of Marriage and Family Relations
6116 Rolling Road
Suite 316
Springfield, VA 22152
703-569-2400

Little Neighborhood Centers
1609-13 West Poplar Street
Philadelphia, PA 19130
215-236-8008

Morrow Bay's PARTNERS Program
Police and Recreation Together for New Enrichment in Schools
535 Harbor Street
Morrow Bay, CA 93442
805-772-1214

National Committee for Citizens in Education
410 Wilde Lake Village Green
Columbia, MD 21044
301-596-5300

National School Safety Center
4165 Thousand Oaks Blvd. Suite 290
Westlake Village, CA 91365
805-373-9977

Parents Anonymous National Headquarters
6733 South Sepulveda Boulevard
Suite 270
Los Angeles, CA 90045
800-352-0386
800-421-0353

Stepfamily Foundation
333 West End Avenue
New York, NY 10023
212-877-3244

Systematic Training for Effective Parenting (S.T.E.P.)
American Guidance Services, Inc.
P. O. Box 99
Publishers Building
Circle Pines, MN 55014
612-786-4343

NOTES

Introduction

1. Ann Landers Syndicated Column, *Santa Barbara News Press*, April 6, 1992, p. D-2.

Chapter 1

1. Ronald B. Adler & Neil Towne, *Looking Out, Looking In* (Orlando, FL: Holt, Rinehart & Winston, 1990), p. 197.

2. From a letter sent to World Vision supporters.

Chapter 2

1. Quoted by James E. Campbell in "Latchkey Children", Child Safety Curriculum Standards (Malibu, CA: Pepperdine University, 1991), p. 2, from the National Research Council publication, *Who Cares for America's Children: Child Care Policy for the 1990s*, eds. Cheryl D. Hayes, John L. Palmer, Martha J. Zaslow (Washington, D.C., National Academy Press, 1990).

2. Dr. T. Berry Brazelton, "Working Parents," *Newsweek*, February 13, 1989, p. 66.

3. Ted Schwarz, *Protect Your Home and Family* (New York: Arco Publishing, Inc., 1984), pp. 4-5.

4. Lynette Long and Thomas J. Long, *The Handbook for Latchkey Children and Their Parents* (New York: Berkeley Books, 1984).

5. Brazelton, "Working Parents," p. 68.

6. Ibid. p. 70.

7. Ibid. pp. 67-70.

Chapter 3

1. William W. Treanor, Marjolijn Bijlefeld, 2nd ed., *Kids and Guns: A Child Safety Scandal*, Washington, D.C., The American Youth Work Center and The Educational Fund to End Handgun Violence 1989), p. 3.

2. *Weapons in School*, National School Safety Center (Malibu, CA: Pepperdine University, 1990), p. 3.

3. David Freed, "L.A. County Found Armed and Dangerous," *Los Angeles Times*, Sunday, May 17, 1992, p. A1.

4. Authors' case study.

5. Authors' case study.

6. CBS special, "Verdict." aired July 5, 1991.

7. Treanor, William W. and Bijlefeld, *Kids and Guns, A Child Safety Scandal,* p. 15.

8. *A Parent's Guide to Gun Safety,* (Washington, D.C.: National Rifle Association Education and Training Division, 1988).

9. Treanor and Bijlefeld, *Kids and Guns,* pp. 8-9.

10. *My Gun Safety Book,* (Washington, D.C.: National Rifle Association of America Education & Training Division).

11. Treanor and Bijlefeld, *Kids and Guns,* p. 18.

12. Ibid.

Chapter 4

1. *Let's All Work to Fight Drug Abuse,* p. 2. Distributed by L.A.W. Publications, 4560 Beltline Road, Ste. 300, Dallas, TX 75234.

2. *Consumer Health Advocate* Consumer Services Group of Blue Cross of California, Spring, 1991, p. 2.

3. *School Safety Update,* National School Safety Center News Service, Malibu, CA, Pepperdine University, February, 1992, p. 1.

4. *Consumer Health Advocate,* p. 2.

5. *School Safety Update,* p. 3.

6. *Consumer Health Advocate,* p. 2.

7. Claire Costales with Jo Berry, *Alcoholism: The Way Back to Reality* (Ventura, CA: Regal Books, 1980), p. 25.

8. "Dear Abby," Syndicated column, *Los Angeles Times,* May 5, 1991, p. E9.

9. Authors' case study.

10. Authors' case study.

11. *School Safety Update,* p. 1.

12. Ibid., p. 2.

13. Ibid., p. 3.

14. Loretta Middleton and Christine Campbell, "Substance Abuse," The National School Safety Center, *Child Safety Curriculum Standards* (Malibu, CA: Pepperdine University, 1991), chap. 11.

15. *Let's All Work to Fight Drug Abuse,* p. 26.

Chapter 5

1. *The Right to Safe Schools: A Newly Recognized Inalienable Right,* National School Safety Center (Malibu, CA: Pepperdine University, 1988), p. 1.

2. Authors' case study.

3. Authors' case study.

4. Stuart Greenbaum, Brenda Turner, and Ronald D. Stephens, "Bullying," *Child Safety Curriculum Standards* (Malibu, CA: Pepperdine University, 1991), pp. 1, 2.

5. Ibid., p. 6.

6. Ibid., pp. 2, 3.

7. *School Bullying and Victimization*, National School Safety Center (Malibu, CA: Pepperdine University), p. 7.

8. "Bullets & Bayonets," *School Safety Update, National School Safety Center News Service*, December, 1991, p. 2.

9. Dr. Dan Olweus, "Schoolyard Bullying—Grounds for Intervention," *School Safety*, Fall 1987, p. 7.

10. Ibid., p. 10.

11. Stuart Greenbaum, Brenda Turner, and Ronald D. Stephens, *Set Straight on Bullies*, National School Safety Center (Malibu, CA: Pepperdine University, 1989), p. 63.

12. Ibid.

13. Leonard D. Eron, "Aggression Through the Ages," *School Safety*, Fall 1987, p. 12.

14. *School Bullying and Victimization*, p. 5.

15. Ibid.

16. "Bullies a High Risk for Crime—Study", *The Sacramento Union*, August 17, 1985.

17. Report at the "Schoolyard Bully Practicum," Harvard University, 1987.

18. As quoted in *School Bullying and Victimization*, NSSC Resource Paper, National School Safety Center (Malibu, CA: Pepperdine University, Sept. 1990), p. 32.

Chapter 6

1. Authors' case study.

2. "Street Gangs Are Big Business," *The Executive Educator*, July 1990.

3. *Gang Assessment Tool*, developed by The National School Safety Center Mailbu, CA: Pepperdine University.

4. Lilia(Lulu) Lopez and Ronald W. Garrison, *"Gangs," The National School Safety Center, Child Safety Curriculum Standards* (Malibu, CA: Pepperdine University, 1991), pp. 3-4.

5. David Augsburger, *Caring Enough to Hear and Be Heard* (Ventura, CA: Regal Books, 1982), pp. 11-12.

6. Adapted from Lopez and Garrison, "Gangs." p. 1.

7. *"Gangs in Schools,"* National School Safety Center (Malibu, CA: Pepperdine University, 1990), p. 12.

8. Ron Harris, "Youth Isn't Kid Stuff These Days," *Los Angeles Times,* May 12, 1991, p. A-20.

9. "Violence in Our Culture," *Newsweek,* April 1, 1991, p. 51.

10. Ibid.

11. *The Spiritual Life of Children,* quoted in "Children's Notions of God," *U.S. News & World Report,* December 3, 1990, p. 68.

Chapter 7

1. From the newspaper insert paid for by Pharmacists Against Drug Abuse.

2. *Let's All Work to Fight Drug Abuse,* distributed by L.A.W. Publications, Dallas, TX, p. 8.

3. Kathleen McCoy, "Help Your Child Beat Peer Pressure," *Reader's Digest,* May 1991, p. 68.

4. *Let's All Work to Fight Drug Abuse,* p. 30.

Chapter 8

1. Mary C. Sullivan and Brenda Turner, "Teen Parenting," *Child Safety Curriculum Standards* (Malibu, CA: Pepperdine University, 1991), p. 2.

2. "The Unhealthy Facts of Life," *Newsweek* Special Issue, Summer–Fall 1990, p. 57.

3. Barbara Kantrowitz, "The Dangers of Doing It," *Newsweek* Special Issue, Summer–Fall 1990, pp. 56-57.

4. Kathleen McCoy, "It's 4 p.m. Do You Know What Your Teens Are Doing?" *Family Circle,* May 14, 1990, p. 52.

5. Ibid. p. 51.

6. Robert C. Noble, "There Is No Safe Sex," *Newsweek,* April 1, 1991, p. 8.

7. Ibid.

8. Ned Zeman, "The New Rules of Courtship," *Newsweek* Special Issue, Summer–Fall 1990, p. 24.

9. Michael Quintanilla, "Hungry for Love," *Los Angeles Times,* June 23, 1991, p. E-1.

10. Authors' case study.

11. McCoy, "It's 4 p.m.", p. 56.

12. Shayla Lever, "Child Abuse and Neglect," *Child Safety Curriculum Standards* (Malibu, CA: Pepperdine University, 1991), p. 2..

13. Peter Coolsen, Michelle Seligson, James Garbarino, *When School's Out and Nobody's Home* (Chicago: National Committee for Prevention of Child Abuse, 1986), p. 12.

14. Diane D. Broadhurst, *Educators, Schools, and Child Abuse* (Chicago: National Committee for Prevention of Child Abuse, 1986), p. 7.

15. Lever, "Child Abuse and Neglect," p. 2.

16. Ibid., pp. 8-35.

Chapter 9

1. Jeffrey L. Munks, "The Troubled Asian Youth: The Deafening Silence," *School Safety, National School Safety Center Newsjournal*, Fall 1989, pp. 27-28.

2. Robert Louis Stevenson, "Foreign Children," *A Child's Garden of Verses* (Chicago: Rand McNally & Co., 1919), p. 40.

3. Louise Derman-Sparks, "Challenging Diversity with Anti-Bias Curriculum," *School Safety*, National School Safety Center Newsjournal, Winter 1989, p. 11.

4. Jerry Buckley, "Mt. Airy," *U.S. News & World Report*, July 22, 1991, p. 23.

5. Ibid., p. 24.

6. Derman-Sparks, "Challenging Diversity," pp. 11-13.

7. Buckley, "Mt. Airy," p. 28.

8. President Franklin Delano Roosevelt, *Address to Congress*, January 6, 1941.

Chapter 10

1. James A. Rapp, Frank Carrington, George Nicholson, *School Crime & Violence: Victims' Rights* (Malibu, CA: Pepperdine University Press, 1987), p. 1.

2. Ibid., pp. 2-3.

3. Ibid., p. 11.

4. Rudyard Kipling, "If," *The Oxford Dictionary of Quotations*, 3rd ed. (New York: Oxford University Press, 1979), p. 300:2.

5. Bert Ghezzl, "Let's Change America's Mind About Porn," *Ministries Today*, March/April 1979, p. 60.

6. William Raspberry, "Teaching Morality," *School Safety*, Fall 1986, p. 6.

7. Ibid., p. 7.

8. William J. Bennett, "The Difference Between Right and Wrong," *School Safety*, Fall 1986, p. 4.

9 Rapp, Carrington, and Nicholson, *School Crime & Violence: Victims' Rights*, pp. 84-86.

10. Donna Clontz, "Victims Can Sue Bullies, Schools," *School Safety*, Fall 1987, p. 32.

11. Adapted from Robert S. Fox, Eugene R. Howard, Edward Brainard, *School Climate Improvement: A Challenge to the School Administrator* (Englewood, CO: C.F. Kettering, Ltd., 1973).

Chapter 11

1. Militta J. Cutright, "Parents Make the Difference," *School Safety*, Spring 1990, p. 8.

Chapter 12

1. CBS Special, "America's Missing Children," aired May 20, 1991.

2. Janet Kosid-Uthe, "Parental Abductions," *Child Safety Curriculum Standards* (Malibu, CA: Pepperdine University, 1991), p. 2.

3. CBS Special, "America's Missing Children."

4. Kosid-Uthe, "Parental Abductions," pp. 3-4.

5. Ibid., p. 4.

6. Jerri Smock, "Non-Family Abductions," *Child Safety Curriculum Standards* (Malibu, CA: Pepperdine University, 1991), p. 2.

7. Ibid., p. 2.

Chapter 13

1. David Freed, "L.A. County Found Armed and Dangerous," *Los Angeles Times*, May 17, 1992, p. A1.

2. Ron Harris, "Childhood: Fearing for Your Life," *Los Angeles Times*, May 13, 1991, p. A1.

3. Ibid., p. A29.

4. Ibid., p. A17.

5. David Freed, "Fear of Violence from Guns Alters Many Lives," *Los Angeles Times*, May 17, 1992, p. A29.

6. "Rape and Sexual Assault," Coalition Against Household Violence of Ventura County, Ventura, CA, p. 1.

7. Ibid.

8. Claire Walsh, "Rape," *Child Safety Curriculum Standards* (Malibu, CA: Pepperdine University, 1991), p. 2.

9. Ibid.

10. Ibid.

11. Ibid.

12. Jim Hoppe, "Sexual Assault on Campus," *The Scroll*, Winter 1992, pp. 6-9.

13. Robin Abcarian, "Jenny's Story: Parents Were the Last to Know," *Los Angeles Times*, October 13, 1991, p. E14.

14. Author's case study.

15. Adapted from "Rape and Sexual Assault," material from The Coalition Against Household Violence of Ventura County, p. 1. Used by permission.

16. *Sexual Assault Prevention Handbook* (Sacramento, CA: Crime Prevention Center, Office of the Attorney General, 1983), pp. 5-6.

About the Authors

Dr. S. Rutherford McDill is a clinical psychologist/family therapist practicing in Southern California. In practice since 1974, his activities include those typical of the spectrum of the general private practice in addition to which he has founded six church-based nonprofit counseling centers, as well as a freestanding nonprofit training center for family therapists. He has written another book on domestic violence as it is found in the Christian community. He is married to (and co-author on other book projects with) Linda—a sociologist teaching at Moorepark College—with whom he shares two wonderful, if not exhausting, daughters, Erin (in college) and Lindsay (in high school) with whom he is well pleased.

His clinical work includes extensive criminal and forensic elements and components which bring him daily into contact with the kinds of individual and family situations addressed in this book.

He teaches at both the undergraduate and graduate levels.

Dr. Ronald Stephens currently serves as executive director of the National School Safety Center. His past experience includes service as a teacher, assistant superintendent, and school board member. Administrative experience includes serving as a chief school business officer and as vice president of Pepperdine University.

His undergraduate and graduate degrees are in the field of business management. He received his doctorate from the University of Southern California. Dr. Stephens holds the California teaching credential, administrative credential, and the Certificate in School Business Management.

As a student he served as student association president of both his high school and university. He was named to Who's Who in the West and Who's Who in American Education. Dr. Stephens has appeared on every major television network including "The Today Show," "Good Morning America," "Oprah," "Donahue," and CNN.

Dr. Stephens serves as consultant and frequent speaker for school districts, law enforcement agencies, and professional organizations nationwide. Additionally, he serves as the executive editor of *School Safety*, America's leading school crime prevention newsjournal. His career is distinguished by military service in Texas and Vietnam. He is married and has three children.